To: T[illegible] Singh

Thank you f[illegible]
gift on behalf of other
women. I believe we are
able to build our communities
together in love.

May this Stories encourage
you and many more.

Together we say
"No to Racism and Hate
No to Discrimination and
Abuse"
But Yes to building our
Country together with Love
and respect of one another

Thank you.

Portia Manzini

sarahportia.manzini@yahoo.ca

Petunia Bolwe
petuniabolwe8@gmail.com

Praise for *Courage, Change, & Faith*

Courage, Change, and Faith; is a very inspirational book that will revolutionize your life and encourage you to be the leader of influence God created you to be. After reading this insightful book by these great women of faith, I must say that I was so inspired and encouraged by their life stories and testimonies of trials and triumphs experienced and shared by each author.

This book is a masterpiece, and I do not doubt it will inspire any reader to rise and step into their destiny. I strongly recommend this book to anyone going through challenges and trials or experiencing obstacles in life. I assure you that through this powerful book, you will discover that conflicts or challenges come to create new opportunities in your lives. Furthermore, you will find tools to help you overcome any challenge you may be facing and reach your destiny.

Dr. KAZUMBA CHARLES Th.,D
Kingdom Insight TV (KiTV Network)
Founder/President
Canada
www.kitvnetwork.com / www.kitvondemand.com

I am proud of the sisterhood that has written this beautiful book. It is great to witness a movement of soulful women aimed to help shift people from the competition, comparison, judgement and jealousy to respect, love, unity and compassion, a movement that champions each other's strengths, celebrates each other's wins, and shoulders together life's disappointments.

Sisterhood is a universal movement inclusive of women of all backgrounds, ages and social status. It says you belong here, and your story matters.

CHAR QUIRING
Executive Director
Sisterhood Ministries Canada Inc.

I support all women in leadership and applaud the Black Women Leaders SK for sharing their stories to inspire and encourage others at a time when society needs more women to take on leadership roles in all sectors.

MAYA KANIGAN
Founder & President
Women in Leadership Foundation

I am pleased to recommend the book *Courage, Change, and Faith: Inspiring Narratives of Black Women Leaders*. As a person of colour, it is our experience to work twice as hard in inequitable environments. By writing this book, these women have demonstrated perseverance to become victors instead of victims despite these inequities. I am inspired by the courage and commitment of these women's leadership stories to empower other women, especially the younger generation of leaders. The book of Proverbs 11:16 says: "A gracious woman attains honour." Thank you for your bravery in sharing your stories so that others may learn and grow.

CAROL LAFAYETTE-BOYD
Executive Director
Saskatchewan African Canadian Heritage Museum

I recognize the tremendous contribution of these diverse Black women who have shared their stories, experiences, strategies and tools for success to inspire and motivate the next generation. The content of this book is a great example of strength and resilience, which brings hope to others and advances the work on authentic inclusion and equality.

HILDA FANKAH-ARTHUR
President/Founder
Center for Intellectual Excellence (CeFIE)

Black women have always turned for support and inspiration to one another, and this collection of thirteen stories from Black women in Saskatchewan and Alberta provides local versions of that larger truth. Importantly, it does so in the words of the women who have lived those stories. The book presents much-needed models for overcoming racism, sexism, and other obstacles that Black women can face in their work and broader lives, while the three watch-words on the road to success these writers have travelled—courage, change, and faith—help map the route for others. The narratives indicate that those who follow these leaders will need the courage to try and try again when confronting the old obstacles of injustice and of daunting new challenges that some will encounter, a vision for the changes necessary to secure justice, and the faith that both consoles in the face of setbacks and uplifts spirits when hopes are dashed. This is a book to be grateful for because when Black women lift their voices, they have much to teach us, whether or not we are Black and whether or not we are women.

SUSAN GINGELL
Professor Emerita
(English and Women's Gender Studies)
University of Saskatchewan

COURAGE CHANGE & FAITH

INSPIRING NARRATIVES OF BLACK WOMEN LEADERS

Courage, Change & Faith: Inspiring Narratives of Black Women Leaders

Published in Saskatoon, Saskatchewan, by the authors listed above, under their groups' name Black Women Leaders. This book may be purchased in bulk for educational, business, fund-raising, or sales promotional use. For information, email us bwlsk22@gmail.com.

Cover, layout and interior design: Theodora Ofosuhima
Proofreader: Kaylin Flowers
Cover and interior photos: Karyn Kimberley Photography

ISBN: 978-1-7388813-2-1 (eBook)
ISBN: 978-1-7388813-1-4 (Paperback)
ISBN: 978-1-7388813-0-7 (Hardcover)

Printed in North America

To
everyone trying to find their voice.

ACKNOWLEDGEMENTS

This project wouldn't have come far if it wasn't for the women behind Black Women Leaders Saskatchewan (BWLSK). Each one brought their talents and expertise to the table. Paula, Theodocia and Bukola took the lead on social media and marketing. Johaine, Portia and Halima were our financial management team leaders. Hannah, Isabelle and Oyin were our editing and publishing oversight team leaders. Rose, Josephine and Petunia were our fundraising team leaders. Betty Mutwiri was the lead author and project lead.

Thank you to Karyn Kimberley Photography for sharing your creativity with us and capturing the amazing portraits. Also, thank you to Theodora Ofosuhima from Obaahima Publishing for designing this book.

Our heartfelt thanks to the following people for their contribution and support: CECS Conseil Economique et Cooperatif de la Saskatchewan, PGI Printers, Veronique Loewen, Verolingo Communications, Benjamin Omoruyi, Barrister & Solicitor, Omoben Law Office Prof. Corp, Talayah's Southern Grill, Authentic Soul Food, Jasmyn Pingue, Tina Bolwe, Siloe Kumbu, Dr. Idy Chukwu and Global Pot.

THE AUTHORS

Rose Kumbu
Petunia Bolwe
Theodocia Quagraine
Josephine Nsimire Rwankuba
Portia Sarah Manzini
Halima Lama Mela
Hannah Ngozi Eby Chukwu
Betty Mutwiri
Paula Collins-Pingue
Isabelle Dena
Bukola Udefiagbon
Johaine Thomas-Miranjie
Oyin Steve

BLACK
WOMEN
LEADERS
Saskatchewan

OUR PURPOSE

We are a diverse group of women who immigrated from Africa, the Caribbean, and USA and now live, work, and play in Saskatchewan and Alberta.

In *Courage, Change & Faith*, our collaborative book project, we were inspired to write our personal leadership stories to inspire peers and the next generation of leaders to maximize their potential by harnessing their strengths, values, and identity.

We aim to contribute to a diverse and inclusive community by sharing our unique experiences and motivating readers to embody courage and faith as they embrace change.

Connect with us on
Instagram: @blackwomenleaderssask
Facebook: https://www.facebook.com/blackwomenleaderssask
Twitter: https://twitter.com/blkwomenleadsk
Linkedin: https://www.linkedin.com/company/black-women-leaders-sask

Website: www.blackwomenleaderssask.com

Black Women Leaders

CONTENTS

CONTENTS

FOREWORD

In an age where leadership has been called into question across the world, where young people are concerned about the futures their parents are leaving them, and where the systems we have followed for decades are no longer meeting our needs, a group of thirteen women came together to share their leadership journeys, laying the groundwork of hope for those who read their book. They are deep, personal, poignant, eye opening, authentic, at times humorous reflections of real women.

Over the years, women have been quietly but consistently moving forward, moving the dial an inch at a time. We often speak of standing on the shoulders of those who have gone before—women who have made it possible for more women to pull the world forward, just that little bit more, sometimes resulting in a giant step but often nudging and pushing with consistent strength. We still don't see the work they are doing as loudly and proudly as we should but, nonetheless, the work continues and the results are more visible with each step.

Black Women have had to work even harder to be seen, to tell their truth, to have their full opportunity to make change in the world. It hasn't stopped them—in fact—it has resulted in even higher truths being told and amazing leaders being created.

These thirteen stories are powerful, personal, hope-inspiring and incredibly important. They will help us understand the impact that diverse thought, approaches, cultures, business practices and leadership styles bring to a community. We aren't there yet. We do not yet fully understand the richness and strength that diversity brings.

And we need to.

It. Is. Time.

Honoured to support these women and the impact they are having.

Monica Kreuger
Founder/CEO Global Infobrokers Inc.
Home of the Praxis School of Entrepreneurship

INTRODUCTION

"I can't do this! I can't write! I feel so vulnerable writing my story."

This was a common sentiment echoed by us. We are thirteen authors from diverse ethnic backgrounds, united in a shared purpose to amplify our leadership contributions to inspire the next generation. Our narratives—of courage, change, and faith—highlight the trials and triumphs we have experienced on our journey and the impact we have made. As you will see, we have navigated significant life changes and challenges with a growth mindset, summoning our faith and courage in uncertain and complex situations. We wanted to elevate the leadership stories of Black women, which are often limited, intentionally excluded or untold within the dominant culture.

Capturing our narratives in print was a practical way to invite others into our lives as a bridge for building cross-cultural understanding and inspiring the next generation of leaders.

We met in the summer of 2020 in a leadership development program for Black Women Leaders hosted by Global Empowerment Initiative for Women Inc. (GEIWI). The program affirmed each woman's leadership potential, purpose and power and inspired *Courage, Change & Faith*, our collaborative book project. We leveraged our talents and strengths to advance the various aspects of the project, which was a remarkable demonstration of collective leadership.

Our relationship blossomed into a real sisterhood committed to mutual support, care and commitment to seeing each other flourish. Our shared values of respect, accountability, professionalism and focus provided a clear compass for our conduct. We have all grown from working together and can attest to the wisdom of the African proverb, "If you want to run fast, go alone; if you want to run far, run together."

We hope that the lessons shared in this book will expand your perspective, enhance your curiosity and inspire you to lead your most authentic life.

With gratitude,
Social Media and Marketing Team—Paula, Theodocia and Bukola
Financial Management Team—Johaine, Portia & Halima
Editing and Publishing Oversight Team—Hannah, Isabelle and Oyin
Fundraising Team—Rose, Josephine and Petunia
Lead Author and Project Lead—Betty Mutwiri

Black Women Leaders

Meet The Author

Johaine Thomas-Miranjie is the President and CEO of JTM Business Solutions, an independent accounting firm. She is also the Co-founder of JTM Foundation, a Canadian registered non-profit organisation with a mission to foster and support the educational development of youth in Guyana.

Johaine is a proud Guyanese-Canadian, wife, mother, and a Chartered Professional Accountant (CPA) with over twenty years of accounting experience. She also serves as an active volunteer Board member supporting other non-profit organisations. She is amongst the first Board members of the Black Professionals and Entrepreneurs of Saskatchewan Inc. (BPES).

Prior to establishing JTM Business Solutions, she served in various industry roles such as Controller and CFO through which she garnered a wealth of knowledge and experience. Her professional track record is marked by strong leadership with a focus on empowerment and growth. She uses her skills, knowledge and experience in accounting and business to empower her team and those in her sphere.

Johaine Thomas-Miranjie

CPA, CMA

"

RELENTLESSLY PURSUING MY HIGHEST POTENTIAL, ENCOURAGING AND EMPOWERING OTHERS ALONG THE WAY

— Johaine Thomas-Miranjie

Chapter 1

PURPOSE-DRIVEN

by Johaine Thomas-Miranjie

Prelude

The day before my sixteenth birthday, the day before I was about to start university, I found myself sitting under a tree in the backyard as I often would, enjoying the peaceful bliss of the moment. The warmth of Guyana's sun caressing my skin along with the soothing light breeze provided the perfect conditions to daydream. I planned to finish my studies by age twenty, land a great job, get married, have my three kids by age thirty, and live happily ever after. It was a perfect plan, complete with timelines!

Dreams Do Come True

I finished my bachelor's degree program a few months shy of my twentieth birthday. I got engaged to my fiancé on my graduation night. Right away, I was hired by the company where I did my work placement, Banks DIH Limited—one of Guyana's leading beverage and food manufacturing companies. We built our house, I married my prince charming, moved into our new home on our wedding night, and had our first child, Brandon, all within two years. Operation life on track was going great. With plans moving forward as I had envisioned, I started to look a few years ahead, and sadly, the vision beyond this point was seemingly uneventful. There were no real opportunities that excited me or goals that propelled me. Life was good, without complaints, but I knew I would be bored if I didn't get something else going. I thought about buying a car and learning to drive. After that, life would have continued as usual, and I would have gone to work for the next forty years until I retired. Great life, but just not for me.

The Journey to Opportunity

One day, whilst my husband was reading the newspaper, he came across an advertisement about immigrating to Canada by self sponsorship. We discussed it and decided to go for it. Less than a year after starting the process we landed in Canada, that was late March 2004. We arrived in Saskatoon, my husband, our twenty months old son and my six-months-pregnant-self, dressed in capris and short sleeves. I could barely get off the plane after sitting so long in the pricey confined space. As we emerged from the plane, me waddling at the slowest pace possible, we looked down from the upper area of the airport and saw an old Black man and a spritely looking Caucasian lady expectantly looking up. They had to be our hosts Mr. & Mrs. Noble, my dad's estranged stepfather and his new wife… my step-grandmother? Complicated, I know.

As we were walking towards the baggage claim area, I looked outside the airport, and all I could see was white. The wind was howling. I turned to Mrs. Noble and asked, "What is happening outside?"

"That's a blizzard." She responded. I nodded as if I knew what that meant. Then, accompanied by Mrs. Noble, Brandon and I took seats in the baggage claim waiting area. Back then, it was just one corner of the Saskatoon airport, not quite an area.

Meanwhile, my husband and Mr. Noble went to the carousel to identify and retrieve our bags. Then, bags in hand, we were ready to go outside to get to the Noble's vehicle. To say that it was quite a shock is an understatement. Had I known better, I would have checked the weather before we left Guyana, when we landed in Toronto and every five minutes after that. Had I checked, who knows, perhaps the story would have been quite different; maybe we would have decided against moving to Canada.

We survived the first shock.

We started our life here in Saskatoon under the hospitality of Mr. and Mrs. Noble, who were happy to have us. My family shared their two-bedroom apartment where my husband, son, and pregnant me slept in one bed. Two short weeks later, Mr. Noble complained of sharp pains, and he passed away within a matter of days following hospitalization. It was all too quick. We were starting to settle in and get to know him. My husband got a job within a few weeks. Shortly after Mr. Noble's funeral, we moved into our own apartment next door. Eventually, we saved up $2,500, enough for our first car, a 1984 Chevrolet Cavalier. I gave birth to our daughter. All of this is under four months of being in Canada. We named our daughter Laura-Lee, after her great-grandmother. As you may have guessed, life was on a different track.

Starting life in Canada took work, but we were happy. Mostly, we missed our families. Our first winter was brutal; the heat in the car worked, but only after you drove for about an hour before it would kick in. In other words, the heat didn't work, but the car did, and we were thankful. It was a step up from my husband having to take two buses to work and us walking to the grocery store and using the stroller to cart groceries home.

The Etiquette of Hard Work and Discipline

About six months after giving birth, I felt ready to return to work. Given my accounting experience and qualification, I picked up the phone book. "Oh wait, what's a phone book? You're wondering." Well, a phone book is an ancient thing that was published annually, a thick, usually yellow book with names, phone numbers, and sometimes addresses of individuals and businesses.

I selected the top five accounting firms in Saskatoon and sent them applications. Shortly after, I was hired by KPMG in the Risk Advisory Department. At the time, I didn't realize how fortunate I was to have landed this job as a new immigrant. The job was great, and with two incomes, things improved financially. With both of us working, it wasn't long before we purchased our first home in 2005—a year after arriving in Canada.

There were so many wonderful people along our journey, at church and work, people who remain dear in our hearts to this day. I particularly remember Elena Harmon. Before we purchased our car, despite having young kids of her own, she would regularly come to pick us up at the apartment, take us grocery shopping, and then back home. Then there was Lynsey Glubis from work; she took her time after work and on weekends to teach me how to drive. My husband couldn't legally because he was not an experienced driver in Canada. I eventually made Lynsey proud, and I passed after my fourth driver's road test. "What a relief!"

After almost a year at KPMG, I transitioned to corporate work as a Junior Accountant at Tron Power, an English River First Nations Company. In 2008, I moved on after a couple of years at Tron. Together with my husband, we began our entrepreneurship journey. Our first business, Exclusive Styles—a designer kids' clothing store—was born. Alongside the clothing store, I provided accounting services to clients under my newly registered Sole Proprietorship, JTM Business Solutions. After over two years in business, we decided to close the clothing store and return to employment. However, I kept JTM Business Solutions as my side job. At this point, I decided that if I was going to continue my accounting career, it was best to get Canadian certified, hence the journey to obtain my CMA designation.

Coming from Guyana, a hard work ethic is inherently ingrained. Fueled by our need to provide and our ambitions for a better life, having to work hard was no problem. So, eagerly, I buckled up, put my head down, and worked. I worked harder and harder, giving just a bit more year after year in hopes that my efforts would be recognized and rewarded accordingly. Years went by, and then one day, I looked up and what did I see? My reality was that the more I gave, the more was asked of me. Whether consciously or unconsciously, as an immigrant, the fear of losing your place compels you to do just that, give more and then some more. So much so that somewhere along the way, you lose sight of what you're giving, where you're going, and what you're getting in return. As an immigrant, it's tricky. You're trying to integrate yet maintain your authenticity, strength, and character. Often you feel lesser than you don't belong, like you don't measure up. As a result, you lack the support network, whether it's the comfort of family or a professional network, both very fundamental aspects of one's journey.

I've always been a strong and confident person. I am fine with hard work, not its complexity or its volume. I thrive in its conquest. There must be a conquest, the achievement of a worthwhile objective, and the recognition of this achievement. However, as I worked day by day, I became increasingly conflicted. Everything got harder, and it was harder to get up, show up, defend, withstand, and represent. I was nearing a breaking point, and worst of all, I was losing myself, my true self, in the process. From the outside looking in, I had a good life, a happy family, a good job, a house, vehicles, and regular family vacations. But, the truth was that I was tired of standing in the ocean, against the tide every day, to maintain self-integrity. I dreaded my days. Nonetheless, I showed up strong. During this time, I started to examine my state of being.

The Importance of Self-awareness and Self-care

Athletes would be able to relate to this. Being an immigrant is comparable to a team qualifying for the Playoffs' final game. You've knocked out several teams to get to this point. Now it's the last game, and you're the away team; you've travelled to the other team's city. The incredible work you must put in to show up at the starting line takes a lot of courage and energy. The pressure, the work, the positive self-talk, it's exhausting. This feeling never goes away, but with time and practice, you learn strategies and gain tools to deal with it. By the way, I'm no athlete. If you saw me, you'd quickly recognize that, but I've watched my son train and compete throughout his soccer career, and boy, do I get it. Home court advantage is a real thing! As you stand there, using everything within you to not collapse in front of the crowd, you hear the words: "Let the games begin!" You are so nervous and fearful of the audience's judgment that your body reacts in unexpected ways, but guess what? It's game on.

I started to examine my feelings whenever I felt anything, both positive and negative. I began a journey of profound self-discovery. The beautiful thing about North America for immigrants is the endless opportunities. You can be or have anything you want. But also, therein lies the deceit. At what cost? If you're not careful, you end up sacrificing the very thing you moved to this country for. I started to recognize the value of my days, the one resource available to me today, with no guarantee of tomorrow. I knew without a doubt that I was no longer truly happy. But the question was, why was I not happy? That was the first of many questions that led me toward true happiness. There were a lot of questions. "What impact do I want to make? What legacy do I want to leave behind? What matters to me?" Beware, this process may cause all sorts of anxiety. It takes courage to honestly examine the situations and circumstances that make you unhappy and unsatisfied. When I began that journey of self-analysis, I realized that somewhere along the way, I had given someone permission to make me unhappy. It took me many years to come to grasp this.

I discovered that I was unhappy because I was giving so much time, energy, care, and consideration to my job at the expense of the things that mattered the most: my family, my faith, and my well-being. I was working harder and harder in the hopes of a better life. Yet, this meant less time with my family, less time doing the things I enjoyed; and I was too tired to enjoy even the time I did have. I was working harder, but it wasn't for the better, at least not by my measure. I achieved my CMA certification but needed more fulfilment, personal improvement, and advancement. Sure, I was working hard, but I wasn't investing in myself (there's the accountant!).

Facing your shortcomings takes real courage. I realized that I didn't have guidance or someone to mentor me during this stage of my life. To overcome that, I had to nurture myself by observing other leaders I encountered, taking note of the good and the bad I noticed around me.

Drawing the Line

At this point, I decided to become intentional about what I wanted to achieve. With that objective in mind, I was very selective of how, where and with whom I spent my time. I became hypersensitive to my environment. I accepted responsibility for my fulfilment and happiness, set my destination, and took a firm grip on the controls to get there. I was intentional in my words, my actions, and my days. They needed to be positive and in alignment with moving me progressively toward my goals. It's incredible how much of our reality we create by what we allow. We've got to take responsibility for what we do in life. It's important to recognize and accept that not everyone wants the best for you. In my opinion, people are primarily concerned with their best interests, and it's up to you to look out for yourself. It's true. The more focused you become, the more this truth becomes abundantly clear.

I have found that life keeps on giving, both challenges and opportunities. How you choose to look at the circumstances you're dealt with dramatically contributes to your general situation in life. For example, suppose we are more intentional in our lives and not on autopilot; then, we will recognize the moments in which an opportunity presents itself to allow us to make our leadership statement. These opportunities are often presented through controversial or abusive situations, injustices, challenges, and obstacles.

To this day, one such situation remains crystal clear. The decisive moment is unforgettable. I was sitting at my desk, and a vendor came into the office expecting a cheque. At the time, I reviewed and approved all payments. True to my nature, there was a system for submission and prior review before it got to my desk. Unfortunately, the documentation for the payment request did not pass the previous steps; consequently, no cheque was ready for him. The vendor became angry and displayed his anger by yelling at me in the open office, expressing how awful I did my job, how miserable I was and a few other hateful things he thought of me. It was so bad that not only did it attract the attention of those in the immediate vicinity but also the attention of my boss, who was passing by. My boss entered the room, took a seat, and asked what was happening. I explained the situation while the vendor continued to vent. To my dismay, my boss did not address the verbal abuse that was ensuing but proceeded to ask me to prepare the cheque for the vendor. I prepared the cheque using every ounce of strength to hold back my tears. Once the task was completed and both parties had left, it was like the floodgates opened, and I could not stop the tears from flowing down my face.

In disbelief, all I could think at that moment was: "After everything I've done and for all that I do, how could it be that this is where I find myself?" One of the team members that witnessed it all came to my side to offer comfort. As she tried to engage, the only words that came out of me were, "I can't do this anymore. I'm done." She was fully aware of how much I had endured in my position, so she responded, "Don't make any rash decisions. Secure another job first." With her help, after some time, I composed myself and left for the day.

As painful as this encounter was at that moment, I later recognized that this person was a messenger. I believed this to be true because this person knew nothing about me, personally or professionally. Yet, he was saying things that hit my core. I received the message that if I didn't like my circumstances, I had to change them! It was time to draw a line in the sand.

That evening I called my husband and kids for a family meeting and explained what had happened. I told them that I was not going to do this job any longer. But, unfortunately, I didn't have a plan. And I had less than a handful of clients through JTM Business Solutions, which I had maintained 'on the side' over the years, alongside my full-time job. The income from these clients amounted to less than half of what I made at my full-time job. Thankfully, my family was beyond supportive; bless them.

At this point in our family journey, we were living on a single income, mine (that's a whole other story), so this decision was not taken lightly. This choice would bring a stark reality compared to the financial stability we had enjoyed up to this point. Thinking back to what I suffered and the months I agonized and wrestled with, this necessary decision still baffles me. The sad part is that this experience was not an isolated incident in my journey. However, through it all, I was mindful to guard my heart and mind because the mindset one chooses to take during a conflict can break or make you. I focused on the positive. Finally, I was going to stand up for my values and demonstrate authentic leadership.

Leaping into Leadership

I decided to quit my 'promising' six-figure job to focus on JTM and fully invest in it as an independent accounting firm. As the single breadwinner, trust me, I counted the cost. Try as I may, I could no longer reconcile my environment and my daily choice to show up and function contrary to my convictions. The bottom line was that I was not happy, and I realized that nothing would happen for me until I, the individual, decided and acted. Personally, this realization transformed my approach to life and the meaning of leadership.

Arriving at this conclusion was one of the most challenging things I've had to do, but everything made sense once the decision was made. It was like I had a new lease on life, and at that moment, I knew, without a doubt, I was doing the right thing. I had to give it all up for what I believed. Through this, I understood that authentic leadership sometimes requires sacrifice. After months of self-discovery, I recognized that I had much to learn about boundaries, stress, self-care, networking, representation, and diversity. Some concepts were utterly foreign to me, while others were about cultural adaptation.

What I clearly knew was my why. I needed and wanted to be in an environment that visibly represented my values. An environment that respects, encourages and supports individuals for who they are, irrespective of their economic status, social status, or nationality. It was on this foundation that JTM Business Solutions, the Professional Corporation, my Accounting Firm, was established ten years after registering it as a Sole Proprietorship and four years after its incorporation. JTM's core values are professionalism, integrity, respect (mutual respect, that is), trust, care, empowerment, and growth. These values guided me as I worked to build the organisation, and a life, which demonstrated that one could achieve a successful business without minimizing, depressing, oppressing, or taking advantage of others. Instead, my goal was to do what I could to help others recognize and realize their full potential while making a decent living.

As It mentioned above, it took me ten years to finally turn JTM into a firm, but now a mere four years later, here's where I'm at: still married and proudly supporting my teenage kids in their post-secondary education. JTM, the Firm, has seven employees and growing. I also co-founded a non-profit, JTM Foundation, with my husband and am an active volunteer board member. I recently acquired a commercial building for JTM, and by the time you get to this line, you'll know I've co-authored this book. Every day I am comfortable with myself, knowing that I am helping others provide, learn, grow, and contribute in their way. I lead by making choices that demonstrate my values. I cannot stress enough how having personal values and goals have helped me in my journey—knowing your why makes potentially tough decisions and choices easy. Then, you evaluate the options based on whether they align with your values and bring you closer to your goals.

Leadership is a great privilege that brings with it great responsibility, which sometimes calls for sacrifice. As a professional and individual, I still feel many obligations to represent my culture, family, and nationality, but I am not burdened by it. I feel honored to stand up for the values I believe in daily. Nowadays, I have such peace in my spirit and joy in my heart. Sure, some days are complex, and you meet all kinds of interesting situations, but I'm grateful and happy at my core. I sometimes wonder, was I working harder back then when I juggled my commitments as a wife, mother of two young kids, a full-time job, clients on the side, and pursuing my CMA designation, or am I working harder now? Honestly, I don't know because I still get lost in it all. Also, I occasionally still experience offences, but a mindset shift has served me well. When someone tries to offend me, it says that they feel threatened in some way by my presence and have decided to go on the offensive. This mindset puts things into perspective, and it's not about me lacking in any way but rather their false perception of me. I sincerely love what I do. I think that's the key!

At this Juncture, This I Know

I am human, wonderfully made, but not perfect. The most significant realization that can guide a person is the humility of the awareness that we are all only human, flawed, despite our best efforts. We need empathy, support, grace, and recognition along our journey. Being a leader is not a position or a title you spend your life working to attain; it's within you, and it's who you are. We are all leaders in our own right; choose to be a leader right now, where you are. At its core, leadership is about courage and commitment. Not about being more than. Start where you are, use what you have, and do what you can now to get where you want to go. In the process, understand that you're not going to be everyone's cup of tea or brew of coffee. Remember, knowledge is power. Know that there will always be obstacles, but your resolve must be to succeed. Socrates said it best: "but first, know thy self." I did the work and took the time to define myself, my issues, and my needs. Through this knowledge, I found my path to fulfilment, and in doing so, I now have more to give to others. Knowing one's strengths and weaknesses is powerful. Know your why and claim your values.

To this end, I maintain my resolve and refuse to live my life by default. I continually strive to be the best version of myself, creating a life by design, encouraging, empowering, and inspiring along my journey. Nothing comes without a cost. To achieve anything worthwhile, one must be prepared to bear the cost. You must value it enough to stay the course and avoid throwing yourself a pity party when things don't appear to be going as planned. Stay committed to your destination but be prepared to take detours. I believe the trending term these days is 'pivoting.' Once I committed to what I wanted for myself, affirmed my values, and determined my measure of success, I remained focused on my goal and adjusted as needed along the journey.

Success started happening when I dared to be my authentic self.

Knowing my worth as a human being and recognizing that I was going to make some mistakes along the way was crucial. Heck, we all do. But I count it all as joy because every challenge I overcome gives me another platform to stand on and move forward from an experiential position confidently. Think of it as skill-building. Terrible things happen all the time and will continue until the end. It's how you deal with them that makes a difference.

Today I am so proud of the woman I've become, in comparison to the girl that used to sit under that tree in her backyard in Guyana daydreaming. I'm purpose-driven and committed to the journey, thrilled to run my leg of this relay called life. I believe I can do all things, and so can you! It requires a transformation of your mind. Outstanding leadership involves recognizing the human in us, and I try to do that daily. I try not to be too busy to identify the needs, struggles, hurts, efforts, ambitions, and passions of others and consider how I can help. Leadership is hard work; leaders get tired, depressed, and hurt. But as a leader, I get up, and I show up. I can't help but think: "Oh, if only you see me." I see you, and what a difference we both can make. I am who I am because of where I come from and the roads that I've travelled, and today in this awareness, I confidently stand.

Some sing in the shower; I cry tears of joy. I'm grateful for every hard step I've taken, for all the happiness I've experienced, all the lives that touch mine, and all my dreams that are my reality today. I cry because I can only hope that I will have the opportunity to give much more, all that is within me to share. I have found my passion, my reason for being, and it fuels me daily. Today my biggest fear is living a life that is anything less than my full potential. Although I am a work in progress, I am doing my best where it matters to me. I am content just as I am right where I need to be. I have no idea where the future will take me, but I know that wherever I go, I will have my faith, family, food, and fun (I mean travel), for without these, I have nothing.

I look forward to the future with great anticipation and joy. I will keep showing up, pursuing my goals, living my values, and creating my best life. Journey with me!

Acknowledgements

Foremost, I thank God for his amazing grace. Thanks to my parents, Frankie and Pamela Thomas, for their sacrifices, love, and support that have contributed to the woman I am today. Special thanks to my husband, Bernard, and my two kids Brandon and Laura-Lee for their unwavering love and support in all my endeavours. I would also like to thank all the phenomenal women that have impacted me and my journey here in Canada, and in particular Piya Sen, Joanne King, Lana Sheppard, BillieJo Dehod and Deborah Morsky.

Meet The Author

Josephine Nsimire Rwankuba is originally from the Democratic Republic of Congo and moved to Canada in 2000. She has earned a master's degree in administration in her home country and is currently taking a master's degree in counselling. She works as a manager in a clinical setting and has an opportunity to identify the missing links in healthcare delivery, where she can be part of the solution.

Her passion is to help people, especially women, thrive and achieve everything they desire. She is a board member of Elim church. She is the founder of "Mushunguri Yetu," a charitable organisation that helps children's education in Mushunguri village, Democratic Republic of Congo.

She is the director of "GEIWI," a Black women's organisation which focuses on helping Black girls and women thrive in Saskatchewan. Her involvement in a mentorship program run by Sisterhood YXE has exposed her to various issues that women face. She has also been mentored by several powerful women. *Courage, Change & Faith* is her first experience as a co-author on a collaborative book project by Black Women Leaders Saskatchewan.

She lives in Saskatoon with her husband, three boys and a girl. She is a proud grandmother of one. She likes spending quality time with her family and enjoys long evening walks.

Josephine Nsimire Rwankuba

YOU DO NOT HAVE TO HOLD A POSITION IN ORDER TO BE A LEADER.

– Henry Ford[1]

Chapter 2

LEADING WITHOUT A TITLE

by Josephine Nsimire Rwankuba

Do a little bit of good wherever you are;
it's those little bits of good put together
that overwhelm the world.[2]
– Desmond Tutu

Growing up in a large family in the Democratic Republic of Congo (D.R.C.), former Zaire in Africa, and being the middle child, I never thought that my voice mattered or that I had something to give back to this world. Now, I know that I cannot ignore how I feel and pretend I do not have anything to bring to humanity. There is something within everyone that only they know and can use to benefit society. Since life is not just one opportunity, but a combination of opportunities, awareness, and determination, I've decided to find those opportunities and use them wisely. So there is no waste in my life; every experience has helped me become the person that was already within me.

The Beginning

I lived in my parents' house for the first twelve years of my life. Later, my parents placed me in a boarding school. I would be away from home for three to four months before going back home for a visit. At that young age, I learned the power of leadership but not in a positive way.

The teachers and the principals mistreated me; practically all the figures that were in powerful positions. I had to obey them without voicing my feelings or ideas. The boarding school, which nuns managed at the time, was one of the best schools in the region. They emphasized discipline in education and spirituality, and for this reason, we had daily routines. Back then, the only way I could define a leader was someone who commands and manages, not someone who empowers.

We had teams of ten students per room with a leader per group. Each leader would get instructions from the nuns and pass them on to their group. I do not remember having team meetings to discuss ongoing issues or required changes for the benefit of everyone. I remember being told what to do and what not to do. As I mentioned before, I felt like I did not have a voice. For that reason, I could not express or contribute to the team. My idea of leadership was to silence others through power. Everyone has gifts that can be used to benefit society even at a young age. Think about a school basketball team, the coach directs the children but always encourages them to be their best. The coach also supports any good idea that a child might share that will benefit the team. Yet, I did not lose anything from being silenced. In fact, even though at that time I saw this kind of leadership as detrimental, in hindsight I can say that through that experience I learned that things can be done differently because every person is uniquely gifted, and they can develop and use their talents for the good of humanity.

As Christ's follower, I found that this concept is described in 1 Corinthians 12:21-22 "The eye cannot say to the hand, 'I do not need you!' And the head cannot say to the feet, 'I do not need you!' On the contrary, those parts of the body that seem to be weaker are indispensable,". If the human body is a single structure with different parts dependent on each other. In that case, society can be compared to that because complex humans form it. Each member is essential for making our world a better place. So, although I could not express myself when I was young, I did not lose the unique gift God had knitted in me from conception.

New Place, New Beginning, New Opportunities

Early in my adulthood, after finishing college, I decided to become a leader who would help others achieve their goals and reach their highest potential. I wanted to challenge myself rather than be the one who hinders people from succeeding. Good leaders can influence people, help them achieve their goals, and attain leadership positions. I wanted to become one of those.

I've realized that life can change once you change your familiar environment. When I moved far from my family and my childhood friends, from our small town, Bukavu, to the capital city of D.R.C., Kinshasa, to pursue my education, I faced the reality of what it meant to be alone and make decisions that would impact my life. I became responsible for my problems and learned how to resolve them. I was in the capital city for my education, but I also needed to meet new people, make friends, and find a safe place to live. It was time to be critical in decision-making. The adjustment took a while, but I managed to move forward.

I discovered the strength that was already within me, but I was not aware of it. I could no longer depend on my high school team leader or my parents for day-to-day decisions. I made mistakes, but I picked myself up and continued my education, and made a new life in a new environment. I discovered that my experience was the foundation for defining my new life. Every day was a learning opportunity. I joined study groups and finally started making new friends. I also encouraged other students to join the groups to help each other in different subjects.

During my time in college, I learned to appreciate and value people. I prepared the study room and reminded everyone of our discussion time. This opportunity for connection allowed me to be helpful in the group. I did not have a specific title, but I committed to reminding everyone about the time and the subject to be discussed. Leadership comes in so many shapes, but the key is to know where you are called to lead and be helpful by empowering others to reach their goals. As Brian Tracy says, "Become the kind of leader that people would follow voluntarily, even if you had no title or position."[3] There is power in a group when each person contributes differently to the group's purpose.

Women and Leadership

> The role of a great leader is not to give greatness
> to human beings but to help them
> extract the greatness they already
> have inside them.
> – J. Buchan[4]

When I finished college in 1984, the Democratic Republic of Congo was not politically and economically strong. However, I was fortunate to be hired in a car dealership within the administration department. I had the opportunity to supervise eight people in my department for ten years. I encouraged the team to express their concerns and ideas on how to improve our department. This interaction allowed me to see how effectively my team could work together to benefit the company. Every human being has the potential to bring change, and for that, people need to be allowed to express their ideas.

When I was in that leadership position, I was reminded of my younger years when I was not allowed to have an opinion when there was a leader in charge. I wanted to work differently with my team. We came up with great ideas, and everyone felt a sense of belonging and being valued. Every improvement that was made was possible thanks to everyone's contribution. My role was not only to empower my team but also to lead by example. As the leader, I ensured that the team knew my values and priorities. Letting them know that the final decision would come from me allowed me to say "no" when some ideas weren't convincing during our discussions. However, I always explained the "why" behind my decision to maintain healthy relationships.

Leaders define the culture of a team or company. Therefore, the team needs to know the leaders' priorities and goals so that all decisions and ideas for the team's progress are aligned with these priorities in one way or another. For example, my team understood the value of collaboration, and I led by encouraging everyone not to focus on their weakness but on their strengths. As a result, the department I led achieved every target needed for the company's progress. My goals were also aligned with the company's goals and having feedback from other team leaders and directors was significant to my team and me.

The Bible talks about different life seasons in Ecclesiastes 3:1 "There is a time for everything and a season for every activity under the heavens." Therefore, I believe there is a time to lead, and there is a time to follow. Valuing my team allowed me to listen and discuss any ideas for the company's benefit with them. There is no leader if there are no followers; therefore, the value I put on my team helped me know when to put on the hat of a leader and when to put on the hat of a follower. Eugene B. Habecker in *The Softer Side of Leadership* writes, "Lead-follow leaders are unafraid to make decisions but usually seek input before those decisions are finalized."

Turn Your Obstacle into Opportunity

> If you do not like something, change it.
> If you cannot change it, change your attitude.
> – Maya Angelou[5]

Life might always surprise us in the way that it calls us to make some changes. My family moved to South Africa in 1991, where my husband found a better job. I moved to this new country where everything was new: people, environment, and language. After working for ten years in my country, I moved to a country where I could not find a job, no matter how hard I tried to apply for different jobs. My husband and I had two young children at the time and, as a career woman, I was not comfortable being a stay-at-home mother for a couple of years. The main obstacle was the language. I moved from a country where French is the official language to a country where English is the official language. I faced many difficulties due to my struggle to communicate with the local people. To overcome that, I started volunteering at a local women association. After one year, I connected with a couple of ladies. Their friendship helped me learn English, and I was able to take a few English classes. As Angelou suggests in her quote, I realized something had to change, and it should be the way I define work. All I knew was how to work for a company.

Gary Thomas, in *Sacred Influence*, writes that "We have to learn that we will never have some of the things we have yearned for, but God will give you ways to develop strengths already there, strengths you may not recognize."[6] The power and strength were already in me, I only needed to use them. My Christian faith has helped me throughout my life experiences. It has always encouraged me to believe that there is always something in me to be discovered. Through this mindset, I found my entrepreneurial fiber and started selling clothing and beauty products. After talking to some of the local women, I learned that there was a need for women's beauty products. My only challenge initially was not knowing people. Still, I stepped out in faith and started approaching nurses at the hospital where my husband was working. It took me two years to expand my small business in the local market.

Everyone has an inner strength that can be discovered when facing obstacles. After three years, I hired three sales ladies interested in selling beauty products. My vision was to expand my business and create jobs in my small town, where it took work for women to find a job. The concept of my business went beyond my imagination when at the end of five years, two sales ladies were able to start their own small business, and I was providing the products. The vision was shared with the team, and they embraced it. Several girls were able to find a job with both ladies. The opportunity of creating jobs for other women was the reward for the risk I took when I reached out to a few nurses at the beginning of my business journey. Being a leader is about something other than having an office or a location, not even having a team of people. Still, it could be making a humble contribution by selling cosmetics to empower women. My perception of employment changed, and I discovered I could create a job. It did not need to be something big but simply anything that would benefit me, my community, and the world.

Family and Leadership

> You were born to lead as mothers and fathers because nowhere is righteous leadership more crucial than in the family. You were born to lead as priesthood and auxiliary leaders, as heads of communities, companies, and even nations. You were born to lead as men and women willing to stand as witnesses of God at all times and in all things, and in all places' because that's what a true leader does.
> – Sheri L. Dew[7]

A family is the most powerful platform to demonstrate leadership skills. Unfortunately, those in leadership in other places tend to neglect the family and put more time into their careers to fulfill their leadership calling. The family reflects society. Therefore, parenting skills are the basis of any leadership. As a parent, you lead a growing team that will impact society. Every leader reflects their upbringing. As a mother, I believe that taking care of the family is the most excellent job description a woman or a mother can have. Family leadership comes naturally because of the connection and love among the members. A mother's responsibility starts early and changes as her children grow up.

At the beginning of our marriage, my husband and I, as a couple, set up our values and defined the kind of family we would like to have. In my situation, even though we worked as a team, I spent more time with the children because of my husband's career, which allowed me to get to know them better and pay attention to their feelings. When my children were still young, my husband and I did some planning, implementation, and follow-up for the benefit of the entire family. We allowed the children to participate in decisions such as what to do on the weekend, meal planning, making a schedule for washing the dishes, and many other chores. We thought this kind of empowerment would help our children express their ideas and feelings better. This practice was essential because I was helping them develop good communication skills and a sense of responsibility by having these conversations. Children have different personalities, tendencies, and attitudes that can be tolerated or corrected.

Be Bold

> Courage is the most important of all virtues because, without courage, you cannot practice any other virtues consistently. You can practice any virtue erratically, but nothing consistently without courage.
> – Maya Angelou[8]

It takes courage to leave your comfort zone and go to the unknown. As a Christian, I believe that courage is a response to faith. Abraham's call is an example, Genesis 12:1-2 says, "The Lord had said to Abram, 'Go from your country, your people and your father's household to the land I will show you. I will make you into a great nation, and I will bless you;'"

We thought we would stay in South Africa, but nearly ten years after our initial move, a new chapter opened for us when my family moved to Canada in 2000. Moving here had its issues. This time it was not the language barrier but rather being part of the minority, which was a new concept and a new mountain to climb. We first lived in the province of Ontario, where we spent seven years before moving to Saskatchewan. As soon as I arrived, I found a support group of African women in similar situations. It helped me understand the power of a community, especially when you are considered a minority.

Canada is a country that welcomes a diverse group of people, and everyone has the opportunity to live a better life. That was the motivation behind every effort I made as a newcomer to understand and find a way to make a living and give back to Canada, our country of choice. My youngest son was born in St. Catharines, Ontario. While caring for my baby, I also volunteered in different children's activities; it helped me connect with young parents and other church members.

My four children were raised in Canada with the advantage of having both the western culture and my African heritage. As a Christian, I also used prayer as a tool in my parenting because I believe I have limitations as a human being, but Christ helps me through every season. Also, I shared my faith and values with my children. My mother used to tell me that once you are a mother, you are a mother for life. I find this to be true. Though my four children are now adults, I still have my position as a leader in their lives. I am still their mother, but my role has changed into someone they sometimes come to for advice; even though they know what to do, they still consider their parents' wisdom. I believe that my leadership has adjusted to trusting my children to make good decisions for their lives and respecting their autonomy.

The family setting is crucial for leadership, and parents should know they are raising future leaders. Kamala Harris said, "Anyone who claims to be a leader must speak like a leader. That means speaking with integrity and truth." These virtues are formed from a young age, and parents have an essential role in helping children become these leaders who stand for what is true and live accordingly. As a mother, I believe that the reward of my leadership is given in the fulfilment and joy that comes when I look at my adult children and their impact on the community. My feelings are beyond any award from any achievement. Leadership within a family is unique because there is genuine love at the center, guiding how we decide and behave as family members.

Preparation is the Key

Leadership requires not only soft skills but also training skills. Therefore, I took the opportunity to go back to school to study Administration. Later I trained as a Personal Support Worker. As a support worker, I supervised the evening team at one of the nursing homes where I was working. My involvement in cultural activities helped me connect with more African and Caribbean people. My role was to help newcomers connect with different people, enroll in schools, show them African stores, and encourage them when needed. I could relate to them, especially the young mothers. I was part of a group of five women volunteers; this was an opportunity for me to give back to the community. I had received help from my community and now, I believed that my contribution was significant in allowing others to achieve their goals and integrate into a new country. Even though I did not have a position, I influenced newcomers by helping them find their paths in Canada. Leadership does not always come with a position or monetary compensation. Volunteering was a way of contributing to my community, and my way of serving in my new country.

In 2008, my husband's career prompted us to move from Ontario to Saskatoon. I first worked as a Health Care Aide for seven years, which was only a simple adjustment since I had worked in the same field in Ontario. I took a few more training classes in administration to change my career, although I remained in the medical field. I have been working as a clinical manager for seven years now. My position allows me to lead a team of twenty-one staff, and I continue to empower and encourage the staff to give their best for the benefit of our community. The staff must know the clinic's vision to allow them to do their work and use their talents. This has been my way of leading. I am not only involved in the secular market but also in my local church, where I serve as a leader of a small Bible study group. I found another opportunity to volunteer in my community within a Black women's non-profit organisation where I serve on the board of directors. I aim to empower Black women and girls to achieve their dreams and contribute to our country.

I believe that there is always something new to discover and as Alice Miller says, "Learning is a result of listening and attentiveness to the other person. In other words, to learn from the child, we must have empathy, and empathy grows as we learn."[9] I recently started a two-year counseling training program to redirect my way of empowering and encouraging others to become the best of themselves. In my many years of encountering and working with different people, I have discovered that we are all broken people and need someone to remind us that we matter. I envision that my new counseling career will allow me to walk alongside those who need help to be able to fulfill their dreams and contribute to society. The world needs everyone's effort to become a better world. Empowering others and believing in each other will help us create that world. My experience and the new skills I am learning will help me navigate this next stage of my life.

Leadership Starts with You

I want to encourage every young girl or woman who feels like she will never be able to fulfill her desires to discover her inner power. She can become the leader the world is waiting for with motivation. It does not matter where you live or come from; you can make your dreams happen as a leader and valued person. This world is waiting for you to do your part in making it a better place to live. Leadership is not only a physical position in society; it also starts within you. The better you lead your life, the better you will serve others. Leadership is about helping others and fulfilling your dreams along the way. I dream of seeing a world where every person gets the chance to fulfill their dreams and make the world a better place.

Meet The Author

Petunia Bolwe is a devoted wife, charismatic mother and a loving grandmother. Twenty-five years ago Petunia and her husband left the sunny country of Swaziland to start a new life in Saskatoon, the city that is known for being the Paris of the prairies. Petunia has always been passionate about being a Sunday school teacher and completed her Child Psychology diploma in 2019.

If Petunia is not perfecting her food delicacies in the kitchen, working on her fitness or spending time in worship and prayer, then she is brainstorming fashion design or putting fashionable outfits together that can kill.

Petunia is a leader in her home, church and workplace and hopes that she can inspire women from all backgrounds to pursue their dreams, soar their wings and fly in their destiny.

Petunia Bolwe

RESENTMENT IS LIKE DRINKING POISON AND THEN HOPING IT WILL KILL YOUR ENEMIES.

— Nelson Mandela

Chapter 3

THE LIGHT AT THE END OF THE TUNNEL

by Petunia Bolwe

Introduction

I am a Black woman who understands my impact in a predominantly Eurocentric society. I am a leader that is willing to evolve and grow with time. I am not just a strong Black woman but also a human with strength and vulnerabilities, hopes, fears, standards, and contradictions.

My mother and grandmother raised me. They were the leaders of our household. My grandmother was loving, generous, kind, nurturing, incredibly smart, and disciplined. My mother was the last born out of seven kids, she was well loved, cherished, and had all she needed. My grandmother was my mother's role model, and my mother followed in her footsteps by being generous to the community members. My mother founded a sisterhood association where she taught the women that joined the importance of motherhood and hygiene. From an early age, I knew I wanted to be like my mother and grandmother. These incredible women have made me into the wholesome woman I am today.

Who Am I?

I am a woman born in Mbabane, Swaziland, the only baby that survived my mother's four stillborn births. My grandmother named me Thshengisile (Jen-ci-le), which means "Showing the greatness of God." I was a miracle baby, so my grandmother and parents were very protective of me. They were scared that they were going to lose me. I spent so much time with my grandmother, so I had a stronger bond with her than with my mother.

I watched my grandmother lead her household and lead the community. I saw how everyone around respected her. She loved cooking and canning pickled vegetables. She encouraged the women in her community by helping them preserve their cultural songs, food, and fashion. She found a genuine sisterhood with these women. She also demonstrated her leadership skills through those activities. In their sisterhood association, they talked about motherhood, hygiene, and how to be a wife. For moments of joy and liberation, they sang songs and danced together; this brought unity and enjoyment among all the women of the community. Sometimes, my grandmother would send my cousins and me to deliver food to those in need. She opened our home to widows, orphans, and anyone that did not have a place to stay. Her charisma and compassion inspired her children and siblings to be more generous toward the community. She was a true humanitarian, a true woman of faith.

A Different Lifestyle in Canada

In my late twenties, I met my husband in my hometown through my cousin. We fell in love, got married, and had a baby. When our oldest child was three months old, my husband wanted a better life for us. So he decided that we should move to Canada. By the time our baby was eighteen months old, we had the documents ready to travel.

I left my family, friends, and my job. I left behind everything familiar to me to join my husband on the adventure to start a new life in Canada. That was a leap of faith. I came to this country without knowing what to expect. We arrived during the winter season, and it was a shock.

Saskatoon was our place of residence. We arrived in winter, and all we could see was snow. I had never seen snow nor felt such cold weather in my life. People were not as friendly and welcoming as people back home. It was a culture shock. I had a hard time forming new friendships. I felt like I didn't belong. I came from a place where Black people were the majority, but in Canada, I became a minority. It felt lonely and scary.

After going through a season of being homesick, sad, and feeling different, God sent my neighbor to tell me about Elim Church. It was a breakthrough because I finally found a diverse and accepting community. My family and I made Elim our home church because it exhibited the love of Christ. I am grateful for the community that helped me overcome sadness and loneliness.

Becoming a Leader in the Church

Over the years, while attending Elim church, I found myself growing as a person. My children attended Sunday school and youth group. I became a Sunday school teacher, a role that I still cherish to this day. I enjoy working with children. As a leader, I feel delightfully overwhelmed when I think about how God develops different gifts and characters for each child. Every child expresses themselves differently. One child may want hugs, while another might want you to listen about how much they love purple. As a leader to these precious creations of God, my role is to be a teacher and a stimulator. It is my passion to work with children. I want to leave a legacy and sow a seed to the next generation, leaving a memorable mark. I have a diploma in child psychology, which allows me to work with children in many ways. I understand and communicate with them as they develop their personalities and character. Each child needs to feel heard and seen. Knowing they are not alone or ignored gives them a sense of confidence.

I am also an elder in the church. This leadership role is allowing my spiritual life to blossom and changing my life for the best. The group of elders has become my second family, and I can form beautiful relationships. As an elder, I must be compassionate and selfless. This role humbles me in many ways. Getting involved in the community and supporting people that attend the church gives me a sense of purpose.

I naturally love to help those around me, and as an elder, it is a pleasure to check on people to see if they are doing all right. As an optimistic person, I love to use this gift to change the atmosphere around me. If I am in a dull or low-energy room of people, I joke to lighten the mood so that I can make the people around me feel good about their day. All of this fills me with great joy.

The Challenges and Successes

As a leader, I have experienced challenges throughout the journey. There have been times when I did not receive the support or resources that could have helped me pursue a different leadership role. When we came to Canada, I didn't have any family or friends to help us with childcare, nor did we have enough finances to put our children in daycare. We overcame this by making some sacrifices. When I went to work or school in the daytime, my husband stayed home with our children. When my husband went to work in the evenings, I stayed home with our children.

Another challenge was losing a job due to a lack of Canadian work experience. Back in Swaziland, I worked in the Ministry of Education with the Exam Council. I decided to pursue the same career path once in Canada. However, the Canadian work system didn't recognize my credentials for their standard of education. So, my first job in Canada was in retail, and since this was my first time working in this sector, I needed to gain the techniques and the confidence to sell. The manager fired me. That event caused me to lose confidence. I became sad because I was financially helping my family with that job. We were worried about how to pay our bills and food. I decided to pick myself up and look for different options because there is always a light at the end of the tunnel.

Initially, it was hard to see any light because the situation was too painful. But my faith in God empowered me to believe that this was not the end and that I must continue to pursue my dreams. So I went back to school to study fashion design and business marketing. Graduation day was one of the proudest moments of my life. I felt empowered on that day.

However, although fashion design was my passion and dream, finding a job was difficult. Saskatchewan only catered to fashion a little. I did not plan to move to another city or province because my family was finally settling in, and things were starting to feel familiar. Therefore. I decided to learn more about managing retail stores and the business behind running them. The purpose was to grasp all the knowledge I could gain and eventually open my own business.

I finally found a job as a store manager in the city. Being a store manager has been the most challenging leadership role I have taken so far. Racism was a recurring theme in my workplace. I often felt that my ideas were invalidated or not acknowledged during some executive meetings. As a Black manager with an accent, there were language barriers with native English speakers. Sometimes I was put down and instantly asked in an offensive tone: "Where did you come from?" or "Can I speak to your manager?" Instead of letting this keep me down, I had to be bold. I had to repeat myself, speak louder and share my thoughts and ideas again and again in the meetings. I learned not to be intimidated but to be strong and to teach people about respect.

On a positive note, being a manager allowed me to be a mentor. I loved mentoring and building relationships with my staff. I gave pep talks to encourage them, and together set goals and budget for the day, this often set the tone for the rest of the day, and the workers put in their best efforts. As a store manager, I hired countless people who did not have experience in customer service. I believed in my employees, so I trained and mentored them. I saw the good in my employees, and with time they evolved and were recognized and rewarded for their work by the company. For example, I had an employee who struggled with the store closing procedure for about eight months. She felt anxious and sad that it was taking her longer than the other employees to learn to close the store. Despite this, I was patient with her and helped her every step of the way. When she finally closed by herself without my help, I celebrated with her because she did not give up. Later, she was rewarded as the employee of the year. This experience taught me to believe in people.

Many of my customers were seniors. They adopted me as their daughter. I have countless stories about the great relationships I have formed over the years. Now and again, although I was the manager, I was reminded to be humble. These people around me were vulnerable enough to share their best and worst moments. As a leader, I want to encourage people because there is always light at the end of the tunnel.

Overcoming the Fear of Becoming

When the opportunity came for me to open my own business, I felt overwhelmed at the start because I lacked resources and networks. I also felt that my business plan was not entirely clear and concrete. So, I put that dream on hold and furthered my education. I went to university. It was exciting and sad at the same time. It was a reminder that my children were still young. My husband and I did not have dependable childcare or a community that could help. My kids needed me. That life preoccupation, added to the stress of juggling schoolwork, proved too much. Unfortunately, I made the hard decision to drop out of university. After dropping out of university and giving up on progressing as a leader, instead of being discouraged, I stayed positive.

Life went on.

One day, a director on the board of the Global Empowerment Initiative for Women Inc. invited me to take the Leadership Training Program for Black women facilitated by BM Leadership Coaching & Consulting Inc. Initially, I had become a leader through life experiences, but after taking this course, the knowledge that I obtained equipped me for my future leadership roles. For instance, I learned about self-awareness which expanded my emotional vocabulary. Before that, I was not able to manage my emotions properly. For example, whenever my daughters and I disagreed, they would talk back to me rudely. That behaviour would trigger something in me which would make me emotional and angry. After the training, I was able to identify the problem or the emotion so that I could solve it or tame the situation before it escalated. I was able to set boundaries for my girls to respect me even if we did not see eye to eye.

Also, from the Leadership Training Program for Black women, I learned that my communication challenges or barriers caused conflicts. From that knowledge, I have learned how to resolve them. In my opinion, conflict is not necessarily negative—it shouldn't be pushed under the rug. Still, it must be dealt with because it is the key to healthy relationships within a community. This skill is an avenue to find solutions for internal and external struggles.

This leadership training has empowered me to pursue my own business. My business will be in women's fashion with a diverse clothing line that will cater to women of all sizes. I will create my clothing line with my knowledge of fashion design and store management and use my creativity to express colour and innovative looks that will inspire women to feel and look their best on their own accord. I am excited to invest my time and efforts to see my dreams blossom into reality. I have learned along the way that God will place us in different places that might be unexpected or unpleasant, but as life continues, we will soon realize that it is meant to be part of the journey. The knowledge and experience accumulated can be applied to a different experience. I have invested so much in my children and my occupation; now it is time to invest in myself. I want to be a role model to my kids and other women wanting to pursue their dreams.

Former President Obama said: "Change will not come if we wait for some other person or some other time. We are the ones we've been waiting for. We are the change that we seek."[10] I like to think that we are all leaders. Whether we realize it or not, we have been serving people in our inner and outer circles, impacting change in their lives. No matter what background one may come from, it does not disqualify the potential to serve.

Meet The Author

Oyin Steve is the founder and managing editor of Immigrant Muse Media Inc., a media and tech company that advocates for immigrants and provides the information, insight and inspiration to thrive in Canada.

She publishes Immigrant Muse Magazine as a solution to the information gap she noticed in the immigration and settlement sector based on her experience as an immigrant. Immigrant Muse also developed immigrantconnect.app—a web app that connects immigrants to the people, programs and resources they need at each stage of their settlement journey.

Oyin is passionate about seeing every immigrant optimize the opportunities available in Canada to reach their full potential. She uses her platforms to advocate against discriminatory policies and practices against immigrants while educating the perpetrators and influencing change.

For her service to the community and contributions to the immigration and settlement sector in Canada, she was awarded as one of Canada's Top 100 Black Women to Watch in 2022 and honoured with the Queen Elizabeth II Platinum Jubilee Medal in 2023.

https://immigrantmusemagazine.ca/
https://immigrantconnect.app/

Oyin Steve

SELF-LEADERSHIP IS THE ULTIMATE FORM OF LEADERSHIP. IT REQUIRES THE DETERMINATION TO KEEP GOING DESPITE DIFFICULTIES, THE DISCIPLINE TO SELF-REGULATE, AND THE DISCERNMENT TO PIVOT AT THE RIGHT TIME.

— Oyin Steve

Chapter 4

LEADING SELF THROUGH CHANGE

by Oyin Steve

Reminiscing

Today is Saturday, October 15, 2022. It is 4:30 pm eastern time, and I'm gleefully preparing to attend the Canada International Black Women Excellence award in Mississauga, Ontario. I am with one of my favourite cheerleaders, Joy, who came with me from Regina. We had both decided to wear dresses infused with our unmistakable African identity. I wear my floor-length royal blue bubu dress with a multi-colour hand-made African fabric, popularly known as aso-oke, embroidered on the neck and shoulders, with a knee-length slit at the front. As I peek at myself in the full-size dressing mirror in my hotel room, I let out a contented smile, knowing that I had achieved the perfect look for the occasion. This is me, an indisputably beautiful African woman with my crown of sleekly moisturized dreadlocks dressed in contemporary cultural regalia that engenders pride in my culture, confidence in my prowess, and faith in my journey.

As I admire the woman I've become, I can't help but look back on the life experiences that have shaped me and led me to this point—one of Canada's Top 100 Black Women to Watch in 2022. Three words sum up my journey in life so far, both in my family life, career, and business: taking **delight** in the everyday nuances of life, adjusting to **disappointments**, **discerning** things that are outside of my control and acting accordingly.

Self-awareness

As a child, I knew I wanted to build a thriving career advocating for something I was passionate about. I wasn't sure exactly how my future would pan out. But I saw three things in it: a happy family, a thriving career, and a passion for advocacy. Unlike me, my dad was sure I would be a successful lawyer, raising a beautiful family. He saw my hatred for injustice and my love for speaking for the seemingly voiceless. He noticed how my voice naturally becomes the loudest in the room when I'm speaking up against the unfair treatment of someone else. A trait that got me in trouble too many times as a child. Being the discerning father he was, he encouraged me to pursue a career in law, and I keyed into his near-perfect vision of my future.

But life had other plans for me, as I was never accepted into the school of my choice to study law, so I opted to study mass communication instead. Although this was not what I wanted, I figured it was better than sitting at home for another year wasting away while my peers were in school. With time, my law dreams slowly withered away as I began to enjoy learning about journalism and marketing.

I was learning about the power of the media to set the agenda for public discourse and to lead to social, political, and economic changes.

However, the more I progressed in my study, the less I became inclined to practice journalism. "Why?" Our professors never ceased to remind us that journalists are usually poor and can barely survive on their income without taking "brown envelopes"—a popular term used to describe a bribe in my corner of the world. An impoverished life was not part of my life's vision, nor was it part of my dad's, and since I valued integrity, I wasn't going to go for a career that constantly tempted me to compromise my values. After my internship as a journalist with a major magazine publishing company, it became even more apparent that I couldn't survive the grit of journalism, so I decided to specialize in public relations.

Stuck in a Rut

I completed my undergraduate studies in mass communications with a major in public relations, married my sweetheart of nine years and got a well-paying job in marketing and communications—in that order and naturally fell into the everyday rut of life. My life was not perfect, but it was good by the yardsticks of my Nigerian aunties. I was less than 30 years old, married and with a good job. Although I was thankful for what I had and lived a happy life, I felt something was missing. At the time, I did not know that I was merely living through the motions without an ultimate goal. I wanted a happy home with beautiful children and a job that paid a good salary, and then what? I had no idea! I knew I could be more, and I wanted to be more. But I didn't know what more I could be and how I could do it. I ventured into a few businesses, but nothing truly excited me the way I wanted.

In 2016, a big sister told me about the new Express Entry pool the Canadian government had just launched for people who wanted to migrate to Canada through the Federal Skilled Workers Program. Up until that time, I never entertained any serious thought of migrating to another country, although my husband had mentioned it passingly several times. After hearing about the new immigration system to Canada and knowing we had a good chance of getting Canadian permanent residency, we decided to try it. We were trying to start a family and knew we wanted to give our kids opportunities to experience another world outside our own. We already had plans to have our kids abroad even though we didn't have plans to live overseas. After all, it wouldn't hurt to have other options. And it wasn't only our future kids who deserved to experience life in another country, we deserved it too, and we reasoned that we could always come back home if we didn't like it in Canada. And so, we began our sedulous pursuit of Canadian permanent residency, which marked the reawakening of excitement for me.

From writing the International English Language Testing System (IELTS) exam multiple times to get my desired score to fighting the crippling system that makes it difficult to access my academic transcript for assessment and everything in between. It was a journey filled with delight, disappointments, and discernment until we hit the climax in 2018. We landed at the Toronto Pearson International Airport as permanent residents with our combined sixty-three years of lives packed into four luggage and a truckload of dreams that our hearts could barely contain.

Digging for Gold

Canada held out to us a promise of a better future with an endless goldmine of opportunities, and we were prepared with our hammers and chisels in hand to dig them all up. From the moment we landed, we began digging for our golden opportunities in Canada by preparing for opportunities. Yes, you can call us gold diggers; aren't we all trying to hit hidden gemstones beyond every surface we scratch? Long before we landed, I analyzed several job opportunities in my occupation to get a sense of the skillsets Canadian employers were seeking in potential employees. I also reached out on LinkedIn to several people in my profession in Canada, joined a professional association recommended by top Canadian employers, and paid to travel to Montreal to attend a global professional conference a few weeks after we landed. Yes, I was earnestly digging for gold.

At first, I was disappointed that Canada's promise of opportunities was a mere fluke to deceive unsuspecting foreign skilled workers into leaving their great life for Canada. I hadn't imagined that getting a marketing and communications job would be difficult. I applied for countless jobs, from mid-senior level to internship roles. I got a few interview invitations, and rejection letters after rejection letters. But I did not let my disappointment stop my pursuit even though the rejection dampened my motivation.

Nonetheless, I discerned that to gain sustenance during the dig, I must find an avenue for refreshment to avoid complete burnout before I hit my goal, or worse still, the kind of burnout that could prevent me from hitting my goal. I went for a two-day personal support worker course and got a job as a caregiver in a seniors' home. There's nothing wrong with being a caregiver; I enjoyed working as a caregiver while it lasted, but I knew it wouldn't last for too long because it wasn't my goal. Being a caregiver in the interim allowed me to take advantage of available opportunities while staying financially afloat and mentally engaged as I worked towards my goals. This is the purpose of a survival job, as immigrants call it, or a transitional job, as those in academia call it.

Three months after landing in Canada and two months after taking a survival job, I hit my first piece of gold. I landed my first role in marketing and communications and bid farewell to survival jobs. Finally, the research, networking, learning, unlearning, and relearning paid off. Many people thought I was lucky to find a good-paying job in my occupation 'just' three months after getting to Canada because, at the time, it was uncommon to get a job in Canada, especially in Saskatchewan, without Canadian education or experience. Many immigrants had to needlessly go back to school to validate their foreign experience in the eyes of employers.

My response is usually a favourite quote by Seneca: "luck is what happens when preparation meets opportunity". Rather than wait for luck, I worked hard until luck happened to me. This is not to say that people with a longer timeline to achieve success do not work hard. Timelines will always differ from person to person and project to project; however, to succeed in any endeavour, you only need perseverance. What matters is that you apply your will every day to achieve your goal and discern when to pivot. If I had given up on my gold digging two months into the dig, I would have failed to hit my goal. Just like when searching for literal gold, there are usually no telltale signs that we're close to hitting gold. Similarly, when working towards a goal, you're never sure when you're nearing your goal, so you must always persevere until you've reached your objective or decide when it's time to move on to something else without the risk of future regrets.

The value of perseverance, planning and discernment came to the fore for me during the pandemic. Did I mention that my job was in the pension industry? At the start of the pandemic, I saw how many people nearing retirement suffered an irrecoverable loss in their pension investments due to the volatile market. These people had planned, persevered, and saw their goals right before them. They suddenly realized they had lost a considerable percentage of their pension pot in a snap of a finger. They had to pivot their plans to either retire much later to save more or retire early with less money. It is critical to understand that planning and perseverance are essential success factors, but we must also discern when it is time to stop and take a turn.

So back to my journey! I resumed my first day of work bright-eyed and bushy-tailed, and it was more than I had hoped, at least at the beginning.

The team at the office was small but respectful and welcoming. I had the most fantastic boss who helped me settle into my role. She answered all of my questions, showed me how to perform unfamiliar tasks, and even patiently taught me how to phrase certain statements in Canada while respecting my unique line of thought. I experienced and got used to the Canadian subtle feedback method through her.

My job was excellent, with just the right mix of challenges and workload, but I missed the thrill of doing something exciting and the stimulating rush of adrenaline when you're about to hit a gemstone when you're gold-digging. Of course, there were times when we'd start new projects that would get me this type of thrill, but I longed to create something I could control and that would continually excite me.

Exactly one year after I got to Canada (I call it my immiversary—coined from two words, immigration anniversary), I was in my office one slow afternoon when I realized that I enjoyed writing and loved helping people. These are two things that always made me feel good. So, I thought, what if I started a blog to share my immigration and settlement journey with other immigrants? I could make someone else's journey a little easier or feel less lonely, or someone could find some delight in what I write. Without a second thought, I went to GoDaddy to get a domain, found the domain immigrantmuse.ca, created my blog on WordPress, shared my first blog post and effectively became a blogger and owner of Immigrant Muse. Yes, I can be quite spontaneous! I loved this name (Immigrant Muse) even though it wasn't my first choice. It identifies me and most of my audience (immigrants) and proclaims what I hoped to achieve with the blog—to ruminate about my life as an immigrant in the hopes of inspiring others.

Pivoting

I enjoyed being a marketing and communications pro by day and a blogger by night. My readers were growing beyond my expectations. Readers were coming back to my blog to ask questions, offer suggestions, share their experiences, and tell me how much they not only enjoyed my blog but also found it quite helpful and informative. Yes, my blog traffic was booming, and I was making a little income from Google AdSense occasionally.

In early 2020, when the pandemic hit and we all had to start working from home, I was excited. Not because of the pandemic but the prospect of working from home and having more time to think about the future of Immigrant Muse. It was still a side helpful (something you do to help people without the intent of making money), but I was beginning to wonder if there was a way to monetize it without compromising my goal of helping people.

Although I was beginning to have some thoughts about the redirection for Immigrant Muse, I was glad that I still had a job that I loved until I got my annual performance review. No, I promise it's not what you're thinking. My performance was excellent, with a few developmental needs, which was great. I even got a performance bonus and a raise. Along with my performance review, I got the salary scale for my role and a discovery that made me question my worth. And that was when I began to experience a conflict of self at work.

I had just discovered that my income was at the entry-level of my role's pay scale. Remember, this was my first job in my occupation in Canada, and before this job, I had a survival job as a caregiver. When I got the job offer, it felt too good to be true. My income increased by over 100 per cent, so I did not consider negotiating the benefits package. I didn't even experience the fear of losing the job if I negotiated because I didn't think about negotiating at all. That hit me hard when I realized I had underpitched myself because I didn't pitch myself.

Do you know why? I weighed the offer and my current income on my judgement scale and determined that it was excellent because it far outweighed my current income. My bad! I wasn't getting the job based on my current income. I was getting it based on my value—a combination of my soft skills, technical skills, industry knowledge and work experience. If I had weighed the offer based on my value, I would have renegotiated the offer and not left over **$30,000** on the table. Having realized this devaluation, primarily my fault, I became dissatisfied with my job. I began to plot my premature exit from the company without trying to renegotiate my income based on my worth and new knowledge—another mistake. At the time, I didn't know I had that option. I thought I would need to get a promotion to be able to negotiate a raise, but since my team was only a two-person team, I didn't see any growth opportunities without my boss leaving her job. But she was darn good at her job and didn't appear to want to leave anytime soon. I concluded that my only option was to find another job.

Now I had two goals in mind. One was to plan the future of Immigrant Muse as a business or, at least, a potentially lucrative side hustle, and the other was to find a job where I could practice all the lessons I had learned from my current job and get paid for my worth.

Thankfully, I discovered the Women's Business Hub, a Saskatoon Open Door Society program that offers training and support to immigrant women looking to start a business. This one-year program, which included weekly in-person training had become an entirely virtual program due to the pandemic. The pandemic wasn't all doom and gloom after all. I joined the 2020 cohort to learn all I needed to know to start a business and test and validate my business idea. Am I glad I joined the program! With the support of the business consultant from the program, I did my feasibility study, drafted my business plan and even began working on registering Immigrant Muse as a Media and Tech corporation. There was a mix of excitement and fear of the unknown, but I wasn't going to let it stop my plan, especially when there was a chance of success. Yes, I planned to transition Immigrant Muse from a blog that provides one line of thought from one blogger to a magazine (with multiple writers) published online and in print and distributed across Canada to advocate for immigrants and empower them with the information, insight, and inspiration to thrive in Canada. Yes, the New Canadian and the Canadian Immigrant, two other media companies doing fantastic work for immigrants, were already in the field, but who says there couldn't be more players on the field? Do you know how many fashion magazines there are in Canada?

On a serious note, my readers were sharing heart-wrenching experiences that needed amplifying, asking questions that needed answers and suggesting policy and program changes that needed consideration. And if I remember correctly from my school days, the media has the power to set the agenda for change socially, economically, and politically, and they can also request information that might not be easily accessible to everyone else. It was high time we used the power of the media to benefit the growing immigrant population in Canada, and I was more than glad to lead or at least be a part of this train.

Also, I had realized that immigrants encounter many other challenges in Canada for which we can leverage technology to solve; I plan to integrate that into the future of Immigrant Muse.

While working on my business plans, I was also actively job hunting. I finally landed what seemed to be the perfect job in February 2021. It was a management role with exceptional benefits. Finally, I got a job that paid me what I deserved, and just like my former job, it promised to have just the right amount of challenges, support and workload. I hoped to gain fresh experience and rediscover myself in this new role.

In March 2021, I started the new job but quickly realized it wasn't what I had expected. Rather than rediscovering myself, it created self-doubt, anxiety, and panic attacks due to unrealistic expectations, misaligned values, and a toxic work environment. After five weeks of trying to wing it without much success, I spoke to my boss about some of the challenges and areas where I needed support to deliver optimum results. To my relief, I was terminated during a Teams meeting the following Monday, six weeks into the job. Although I was somewhat disappointed, I was happy to be free from the toxicity. Moreso, I was not left without income as I was eligible for employment insurance. Even though it wasn't much, I considered it a win-win. She gets to maintain her toxic work environment, and I get to maintain my mental health and self-worth with a little income and plenty of time to work on my new business. Still, I was afraid about the future.

Self-determination

As I sat in front of my 27-inch monitor and stared at my reflection after the Teams meeting, I said a silent prayer and resolved never to let anybody or anything outside my control make me feel less worthy. I echo Marianne Williamson's poem:

> Our deepest fear is not that we are inadequate.
> Our deepest fear is that we are powerful beyond measure.
> It is our light, not our darkness that most frighten us.
> We ask ourselves, who am I to be brilliant, gorgeous,
> talented and fabulous?
> Actually, who are you not to be?
> You are a child of God.
> Your playing small does not serve the world.
> There's nothing enlightened about shrinking so that other
> people won't feel insecure around you.
> We were born to make manifest the glory of God that is
> within us.
> It's not just in some of us; it's in everyone.
> And as we let our own light shine,
> we unconsciously give other people
> permission to do the same.
> As we are liberated from our own fear,
> Our presence automatically liberates others.

A couple of weeks before my termination, I finalized my business registration and received my incorporation document for Immigrant Muse Media Inc. But paralyzed by the work anxiety and stress, at the time I could not do anything about my business.

After I reminded myself of my worth and mission to light my little corner of the world, I went to the bank with renewed enthusiasm to open a business account for Immigrant Muse Media Inc. I had lost a job that was not within my control, but I had the business I could make into whatever

I wanted; I darn well will make it into a thriving business that'll respect everyone's authenticity and advocate for the same.

My husband's income and my meagre EI benefit were sufficient to sustain us for a while, but I knew I couldn't afford to be out of a job for too long. I made a three-month plan for things I needed to achieve for my mental health, career, and business. I exercised and practised spiritual meditation regularly to maintain excellent physical and mental health. I recruited freelance journalists across Canada, spoke with potential partners, applied for funding, and recreated my business and magazine website to set up the foundational Ps for my business—product, people, and process. I also applied for only jobs that would meet my needs mentally, professionally, and financially—in that order.

This journey made me realize that my worth is not measured in monetary terms. While money is essential—we must pay bills and plan for retirement—but I've realized that living my values, maintaining my mental health, having time for my family and pursuing my passion will always be more important than money.

Two months after my termination, I landed a job that offered growth while allowing me time to prioritize the things that are important to me.

In September 2021, I began publishing my online magazine Immigrant Muse Magazine. The online magazine gets more than 100,000 average monthly readers globally. In December 2021, I published the magazine's first print issue, with 1000 copies distributed across Canada to inclusive corporate organisations, libraries, settlement service organisations, community and cultural organisations and airports. My company, Immigrant Muse, has also started a robust advocacy campaign investigating discriminatory policies and practices against immigrants to educate perpetrators and achieve a better outcome for immigrants. We have also developed the Immigrant Connect (iConnect) app that makes it easy for immigrants to connect to the people, resources, and services they need at each stage of their immigration and settlement journey. It hasn't been all rosy. There have been a few disappointments along the way, and I am not where I hoped to be, but I'm making progress, living my values, and making an impact.

Today, nineteen months after I held my business incorporation documents for the first time, I am recognized as one of Canada's 100 Top Black Women to watch. I am receiving an award for believing in myself and taking a leap of faith to start Immigrant Muse Media Inc. I don't know who nominated me for this award, but they nominated me because they saw the impact of my work. I'm not going to downplay this anonymous clap because I know that behind that clap, there are many others whose candles have been lit by my spark.

As I give one last glance in the mirror before leaving my hotel room to walk on stage and accept the award, I hold my head high. I realize that my journey has had twists and turns with sprinkles of disappointments and delights, but I've picked my lessons along the way and discerned my true worth. I wouldn't have it any other way. At this point, my life has the three components that I saw in my future as a child—a happy family, a thriving career, and a passion for advocacy. I'm still young and expect other twists and turns in the future—that's life. Whatever life brings, I'm confident I can handle it with the support of the One who gives me power beyond human understanding. I am that woman I had always wanted to be and more.

"

OUR DEEPEST FEAR IS NOT THAT WE ARE INADEQUATE. OUR DEEPEST FEAR IS THAT WE ARE POWERFUL BEYOND MEASURE.

— Marianne Williamson

Meet The Author

Originally from Kenya, Isabelle identifies herself as a Black African-Canadian woman. She holds a degree in Community Development and a Master's degree in Social Work.

She has an extensive social work background that spans mental health, program, and community development fields. Isabelle's work is guided by using a lens of trauma-informed, cultural humility, anti-oppressive and social justice.

She is most passionate about the intersection of immigration, mental health, and women's health. Isabelle also strongly advocates for equity, diversity, and inclusion in different community spaces. When she is not working, she values, protects, and prioritizes her self-care by creating opportunities for prayer, meditation, gardening, volunteering, reading, and travelling for "ocean therapy" when possible.

Isabelle Dena-Flomo

BA, MSW, RSW, Ph.D. c.

I'VE LEARNED THAT PEOPLE WILL FORGET WHAT YOU SAID, PEOPLE WILL FORGET WHAT YOU DID, BUT PEOPLE WILL NEVER FORGET HOW YOU MADE THEM FEEL.

– Maya Angelou[11]

Chapter 5

EMBRACING VULNERABILITY IN LEADERSHIP

by Isabelle Dena

> There's power in allowing yourself to be known and heard, in owning your unique story, in using your authentic voice, and there's grace in being willing to know and hear others.
> – Michelle Obama[12]

Prologue

If someone told me that one day, I would be able to contribute a chapter about my story to a group book project, I would have never believed them. How could it be possible? I am a woman from a small minority tribal community in Kenya, East Africa! As I write this chapter, I cannot help but have these thoughts cross my mind. What have I accomplished that is valuable to share with others? The constant feelings of not being good enough and second-guessing myself have shaped how I navigate my life. However, I do not let these feelings stop me from pursuing opportunities as they arise. I do it even when I am scared. In this chapter, I want to share how I stepped into leadership roles while embracing my vulnerabilities.

In 2021, I met a group of beautiful and ambitious Black women leaders living in Western Canada and working in various career fields. We bonded over our lived experiences of leadership in different spaces and learning to overcome the challenges that get in the way of success. We then decided to write a book together and collectively share our experiences. We noticed the limited narratives highlighting stories of Black women in leadership circles. I believe there is relevance in the current North American history to amplify stories written by Black people about our experiences using our own words to educate the broader society.

We live in a time that is witnessing a growth in racial awareness about oppression and injustice, hence the current push for equity, diversity, and inclusion policies in workspaces.

On the other hand, when I watch the news and social media, I see Black women are beginning to be 'seen' and are taking up or asked to take leadership positions. Reading about these women is inspiring. Therefore, I felt a sense of duty and honor to be part of this book project, hoping that at least one young Black woman might see herself represented in my story and be inspired to lead.

My Background

My story begins in the Kilifi district, one of Kenya's coastal regions. I grew up in a culture where I heard it was better to educate boys than girls. It was a gendered society with clearly distinct gender roles for females and males. Women were expected to be the caregivers—give birth to babies and take care of their home and spouse. In contrast, men were the breadwinners. That was a culture in which high school education for girls was enough. Most girls in my community were married off after their education. After high school, as far as I can remember, I became educated enough and felt pressure from the community to get married

However, the courage of my mother and father, who refused to give in to the pressure and instead did all that they could, despite us being financially poor, encouraged me to pursue my post-secondary education. I enrolled in a university in Nairobi, Kenya's capital city. This experience opened my eyes to the possibility of dreaming big as a woman. My family and I had to move to Nairobi. Moving from a small community to a big city offered me many opportunities.

Leading While Struggling with an Inferiority Complex

One of my leadership opportunities came after attending a new church for a few years. My peers invited me to lead the youth group and co-chair it. Becoming a youth leader was my first leadership role. I was about eighteen or nineteen years old. I accepted the challenge because I was co-chairing with another person—which meant I didn't have to take full responsibility for the youth group. Sometimes I hid under the shadow of the other co-chair to avoid carrying some leadership responsibilities. I was not confident and struggled to fit in with others. I felt that I was not as affluent as most of my peers. I lived in a different part of the city, and my family came from a humble background. I didn't have the same luxuries as my companions, and frankly, I felt intimidated. I was scared that they might not like me. I could not afford nice clothes, and sometimes my parents struggled to provide for our basic needs. I did not speak English as well as my peers. I have to say that throughout my youth leadership, I led while scared. Even with all my insecurities, I got opportunities to explore public speaking, organize fun activities, and take charge of representing youth at different events.

It was not easy for me because I struggled with an inferiority complex. However, this experience taught me the importance of focusing on my strengths rather than my deficiencies. I know that my peers saw something in me and wanted me to lead even when I did not see leadership skills in myself. This experience gave me a glimpse into what leading a group means at a young age. Little did I know that a new world of opportunities was coming my way.

After completing my undergraduate degree, one of my professors encouraged me to pursue a graduate degree. I thought I was already highly educated with my undergraduate diploma, but this professor saw my potential. I never imagined that I could go this far in my higher education. That day when I realized I could become 'somebody', a dream was born in me. Writing this reminds me that sometimes we are the ones to put up barriers for ourselves or are too scared to go out of our comfort zones. When we leave the places that feel comfortable, we confront uncomfortable or scary things and situations. I can compare this to a butterfly. You only see its beauty when it flies. You don't witness the process when it struggles to come out of the cocoon. The process of metamorphosis is a necessary part of the life cycle to produce a beautiful butterfly. The thought inspired me to leave my comfortable lifestyle—the warmth of my parents and siblings—to pursue a graduate degree in North America. This continent was unfamiliar to me; I had only seen it in movies with its glitz and glam. I was scared to travel since it was my first time leaving Kenya. Through the decision to move from Africa to North America, I began my metamorphosis into the kind of woman I am today. This transition influenced my leadership style.

I never knew I was Black until I came to North America. Perhaps some of you are asking yourself "why?" I was twenty-four years old when I moved to the United States to pursue my graduate studies. As a young woman in my early twenties, leaving my beloved Kenya to pursue my academic dream was a great accomplishment. However, once I was in America, it did not take me long to realize how my skin colour defined me. Suddenly my skin tone became a 'thing' that defined the world around me—academia, health institutions, social settings, and community environments. Being Black was associated with how I was 'allowed' and 'accepted' in these spaces. I struggled internally because of the 'given' identity as a Black woman versus how I self-identified as an African woman. I struggled when people called me a Black woman, because that's not how I wanted to be identified. I just wanted people to know me, the woman behind her colour. I must admit that it was maybe my naivety being new in North America; I was confused about many things. In Kenya, I did not have to worry about my skin colour as most people there looked like me, except for the occasional White tourist. My experience was with gender roles, norms, and ethnic tribes as defining factors in my country. However, it was different in America. I quickly learned to accept my given identity as a Black person. Yet, I struggled with being reduced to a single identity based on my skin colour because I was much more than my phenotype.

I am grateful to my husband because he helped me make sense of my struggle with this ‘new given’ identity. He was already familiar with his experience of being a Black African man in America. I met my husband in Kenya while we were both pursuing our undergraduate degrees. He then moved to America two years before me for his graduate studies. When I finally arrived in America to study, we got married. Due to our growing family and the uncertainty of living in the United States, we moved to Canada in 2009 for greener pastures. Once in Canada, we had our third child. I had not anticipated that the same struggles I had in the United States were also present in Canada. As an African woman navigating workspaces in Canada, I was once again defined by my skin colour.

Confronting Conflict in Leading

I have been fortunate to take on various leadership roles here in Canada, either in my employment or while engaging in volunteer activities in the community. I am a registered Social Worker, and I have been working in the mental health field for the past fifteen years.

One pivotal role in my career as a Social Worker was when I was asked to be a supervisor to lead a team. This role fell on my lap when I least expected it. I had been with the organisation for a couple of years, so I was already familiar with the department’s processes. My organisation’s management team already knew my work ethic, so leading the group was the next step in my career path. Leading was a smooth transition because I had already been in workspaces where I had experienced good and bad leadership. I knew the skills I wanted to possess when I had the opportunity to lead by observing other good leaders. This role forced me to establish firmer boundaries with the group as I was no longer their peer. I now had a set of responsibilities and obligations and a checklist of duties to fulfill as a supervisor within the organisation.

The first few weeks were challenging because my peers had to get used to the idea that I was responsible for the team and that I had expectations for their work performance. As a result, I noticed some friction with some team members. One instance was when I requested that a team member be accountable for their work. I called them out about something they were supposed to do and had not done. This team member became confrontational and reported me to my boss.

We were both called for mediation to resolve the conflict the following day. I was annoyed. My self-confidence was shaken a bit, but I think it was more that I was embarrassed to be 'summoned' for mediation. I was following my organisational supervisory duties. This team member had difficulty accepting that I was now in a leading position. I wanted to prove to the organisation that I deserved to lead the team and was qualified to do so. I did not want this incident to stain my role, be a deciding factor for the organisation's upper management, or impact my performance evaluation. That incident taught me that setting boundaries is essential. Even when the issues escalated to the manager, I was still candid about my responses and interactions with them. I tried not to take it personally throughout the process because I was doing my job. In this role, I understood that a leader fulfills an organization's mission while bringing others on the team to achieve the overall vision.

Challenges in Leading

Taking on leadership roles has been challenging. I have faced various challenges. The first challenge was dealing with ***microaggressions*** at work. I have had people questioning my accent and the way I spoke because I did not have a 'Canadian' pronunciation, and thus I was always visible in that way. Further, people also asked me about my monthly hairstyles and my country of origin. Also, there were invading questions such as: "Where are you 'really' from? Where did you go to school? How did you get this job?"

I felt I had to prove my academic credentials to these people to show them that I was, and am still, more than qualified to be in these leadership roles. These incidents have impacted me as a leader because I am always aware of other people's stereotypes and biases about me as a Black woman. Sometimes, I feel more scrutinized and undervalued, and my decisions undermined than my White Canadian-born counterparts. I am usually the only Black person on the team.

Secondly, I have always struggled with ***feelings of not being good enough***, constantly questioning and second-guessing myself. The issue of an inferiority complex has been a struggle since my youth. This problem followed me into adulthood and prevented me from taking on leadership roles. Sometimes, it made me hesitate to accept a position even when I was more than qualified. I would struggle with these thoughts, "What would people think? Am I being tokenized because they want to fill the gender or minority gap for leaders in the organisation?" And, of course, experiencing micro-aggressions can significantly affect one's confidence.

Thirdly, struggling to balance professional work with the demands of motherhood, having a young family, household roles, and responsibilities. I have had to work later to ensure a project is done, thus sacrificing family time, or missing my children's school events or extracurricular activities. In addition, I struggled with getting reliable childcare for my children so I could work. I am not alone in facing this challenge, as it can be a real struggle for most diaspora women without extended family support.

Finally, another challenge has been not seeing any Black women in leadership at my workspaces. Representation matters! Not being able to see someone who looks like me within the organisation, someone I could confide in and share my experiences with at work, was challenging.

To Be Inspired

We all need to be inspired by someone. I would not have had the desire to be a leader if I hadn't seen or had examples of women in leadership. Marian Wright Edelman said: "You can't be what you can't see." My greatest inspiration is my mother. She gave me my first template of leadership as I observed her in our home. I appreciate how she ensured that our home affairs ran smoothly and kept the family organized. I saw her taking leadership roles in the church by leading and managing the Women's Ministry, speaking at community events, and pursuing higher education to better equip herself for more leadership opportunities. I also saw how she handled criticism with grace, humility, and the wisdom she bestowed on the women she worked with. Through her daily activities, I realized that women could take leadership roles, not just men.

Another woman mentor who inspired me is Betty Mutwiri, an influential local Saskatchewan Black woman leader. Seeing her balance motherhood, marriage, and professional life is inspirational. Betty has allowed me into her life and has given me space to glean from her as she navigates leadership in predominantly White spaces. Michelle Obama also inspires me. During her tenure as the first African American First Lady of the United States of America, it was admirable how she led different initiatives and served as a role model to many.

I am also encouraged by historical African women who fought colonial powers. I am just beginning to know and read about them. These women had to endure a lot to fight colonial leaders and did with the little they had. However, they were able to gather other women and fight. For example, Yaa Asantewaa, an influential Ghanaian Queen Mother born in 1840, was a skilled farmer before ascending to the title of Queen Mother (OBAAHEEMA, obaa-hi-maa) in the 1880s. As the Queen Mother, Asantewaa held many responsibilities, including being the Gatekeeper of the Golden Stool. The Golden Stool is an emblem of the Ashanti kingdom, cultural system, and power. In 1896, the Ashanti people began to rebel against the British presence in their lands, and the British attempted to construct the "Gold Coast" colony. To retaliate, the British captured and exiled Asantehene Prempeh I, King of the Ashanti, and Asantewaa's grandson Kofi Tene, who was also an influential leader. The British removed the king and other Ashanti leaders to the Seychelles Islands to acquire the Golden Stool. While the remaining leaders within the community debated how to best respond to the British threat, Asantewaa held her ground and rallied the troops.

To inspire the leaders of her community, Asantewaa proclaimed that if the kingdom's men would not defend the people, then the women would rise to the challenge. Her courage invigorated the men and challenged traditional gender roles. Her leadership and passion led to her role as Commander in Chief of the Ashanti army to fight against the British colonizers to protect the Golden Stool.

Another historical African woman that inspires me is Mekatili wa Menza born in 1860 in Giriama, Kenya. Mekatilili was an active and prominent member of traditional women's groups in the community, such as *Hifudu* and Makushekushe, which she rose to head later. Following the death of her husband, she had more freedom to move around and rally the people. Mekatilili had excellent oratory skills and her charisma and bravery she led public meetings called *baraza*, mobilizing the men to take oaths and make sacrifices to restore their sovereignty. At a *baraza* in August August 1913, Mekatilili got into a heated argument with the British administrator, Arthur Champion, whom she slapped! Swiftly, the Giriama men rallied to defend their heroine and were ready to deal with the British official who was taken away. However, the British responded by firing shots at the gathering crowd. Realizing their initial miscalculation in underestimating Mekatilili's influence, the British plotted and succeeded in arresting her along with Wanje wa Mwadorikola on October 17, 1913.

I can only imagine what these two historical figures endured to lead their communities in battles and bring freedom against all odds. It is another leadership level to bring a revolution to one's community. These two women did not have any formal education, nor had they attended any leadership seminars that we are aware of; however, they showed determination and boldness in challenging the colonial authority, despite having to endure adverse consequences. Their courage is admirable, and their bravery inspires me. As I continue to read their stories and learn from them, I am encouraged to continue defending a cause worth fighting. As a Black woman, for me, that cause is to continue advocating for social justice and equity in any space and capacity presented to me, whether in leadership roles or others.

Five Important Lessons That Have Shaped My Leadership

Looking back at my leadership experiences, I would say that embracing my vulnerabilities has strengthened me and helped me let go of the shame. Facing the challenges I listed above made me a better leader. In addition, I have learned five important lessons that have shaped my leadership style.

Firstly, being **authentic**. Over the years, I have tried to fit into what society expects me to be. As I have become older, in my early forties, I am embracing my authentic self and not allowing people to dictate whom I am supposed to be to fit in. Instead, I accepted myself with all the flaws. Consequently, this has helped me feel good about myself and increased my confidence. I know my values and my life's goals. I don't have to blend in because standing out is okay.

Secondly, ***setting*** **boundaries**. I used to be a people pleaser. I so desperately wanted everyone's validation that I would do anything to please others at the expense of my emotions. As a result, people took advantage of me, especially in work and community spaces. But when I learned what boundaries were and the importance of setting them, I started incorporating them into my life. Initially, I was afraid that people would reject me by setting boundaries; however, I felt a sense of freedom by doing that. I mean what I say, and I say what I mean. I have learned to say NO!

Thirdly, having a female leader **mentor** whom I admire has helped me shape my leadership journey. In my life, I have been fortunate to meet incredible women leaders who have given me the ‘ropes’ of how to be a good leader. These are mentors whom I seek advice from. And I appreciate when they challenge me in areas where I need to grow. People need to have mentors in all aspects of their life. I think a mentor is someone I can look up to as a role model. She must be someone who allows me to ‘see’ her as she navigates life, somebody who provides a template for leadership that I could follow as I create my leadership framework. I value my relationships with my mentors, and as I am being mentored, I am also in a place I can coach others. I glean from the wisdom of these women.

The fourth lesson is learning to accept feedback. It is humbling to be in a situation where someone ‘checks’ on you and provides constructive feedback. However, I have learned not to take things personally and receive the feedback I get from others, especially my mentors, as I know they have my best interest at heart.

Lastly, the most important lesson for me throughout my journey of stepping into leadership roles is knowing my **worth**. I am still evolving as a leader, and continually learning and reading helps me grow. There are leadership templates everywhere, and I am learning and redefining what it is to be a Black woman leader. I am grateful for the women leaders who have shaped my leadership experiences. It’s upon their shoulders that I stand and lean on because they can, and I can do too. No one can weigh my worth except me.

Meet The Author

Halima Lama Mela was born in Nigeria. She has a degree in Law from Ahmadu Bello University, Nigeria, a Bachelor in International Studies from University of Saskatchewan, Canada and a Masters in Human Resources Management from the University of South Wales, Wales, United Kingdom.

She is a dedicated and passionate believer in being an uplifter and always works on assisting others, especially new comers to find their footing and thrive economically. She is finding her voice in speaking about caring about mental health from a patient perspective and is an advocate for diversity which she sees in all areas of life. She is also an active member in her local church.

She and her husband own Hope Clinic. They are blessed with three sons, their joy.

Halima Lama Mela

LL.B, BA, MSc HRM

"

WHEN YOU DECIDE TO SERVE OTHERS AS A LEADER, THE TEAM'S SUCCESS BECOMES YOUR SUCCESS.

- John C. Maxwell

Chapter 6

SERVANT LEADERSHIP
Leading by Serving Others

by Halima Lama Mela

Introduction: Who is a Leader?

When we think of leadership or what it means to be a leader, we often think of a person in charge of an organization, a manager, or even a CEO. All these are not wrong about who leaders are and what they do, but there is more to leadership than bossing and managing people. As the saying goes, everyone can be a manager, but not all managers are leaders. Leading people takes boldness. Sometimes this role requires the leader to come alongside people or work behind the scenes to see a vision brought to life.

When I think about the vision of *Courage, Change & Faith*—to inspire and empower women to stand in their power, overcome challenges, be bold, aim high, and learn from their mistakes—and the fact that I am contributing to it, I find it quite funny. I was one of those who thought that a leader must have a huge platform to influence people. Leaders were men like Martin Luther King (Dr. King) and Mahatma Gandhi (Gandhi). Dr. King led the civil rights movement in the United States of America. On the other hand, Gandhi led a non-violent protest in India as resistance to fight for Indian independence from British rule.

Honestly, I always imagined a leader to be a person out there doing massive things and getting awards for their work. Whenever someone complimented me as a leader, I laughed it off, thinking: "How can I be a leader? A person like Dr. King—fighting for people's rights—is a leader. A leader is someone with responsibilities, an upright wholesome person." Oh no, Halima did not fit into her definition of a leader! Now, I know that leadership starts when one decides to serve others, and the team's success becomes their success too.

My Background

I was born in Nigeria in a town called Zaria in Kaduna in 1974. I am the oldest of five siblings—two brothers and two sisters. Sadly, we lost one sister in 2014. My dad is a medical doctor, while my mom is a practicing barrister. Mom started as a nurse and later transitioned to practicing Law in 1997. I received my elementary, middle, high school, and university education in Nigeria.

I remember that in my final year of high school in 1991, I was not a prefect—a senior student that can enforce discipline—but just an ordinary student, as we referred to ourselves, "floor members"—it was used lightly as a form of banter. This position was not bad because it had zero responsibility. I also remember a club in our school called Arts and Photographic; it was not popular or as active as when I started form 1 (grade 7). However, towards the end of form 5 (grade 11), I found myself, together with a couple of my mates, actively leading the club and trying to revive it to make it appealing. I never thought of that as a sign of leadership due to my narrow definition of the role.

I overlooked how in my final year of high school, though I was 'just' a floor member, I could help those already prefects to carry out their responsibilities. As I look back, this behaviour was typical. We did not have to be prefects to stamp our mark; we were all leaders—shout out to my classmates, class of 1991 from Federal Government Girls College (FGGC) Bakori in Katsina State.[1] I did not realize back then

1. FGGC is part of the unity schools in Nigeria that is under the federal government ministry of education as opposed to North American schools, which are provincially

that this leadership style was called servant leadership. I found myself in this leadership role thanks to the experience of walking alongside and supporting my mates, who were officially appointed as prefects.

At university, I studied Law and completed that degree in January 2000. I met and married my husband, and we are blessed with three boys. My husband is a physician psychiatrist; he mainly works at the university as a professor in psychiatry and as a clinician, in addition to other clinical work on contract for various groups.

In 1999, after completing my studies in Nigeria, I joined my husband in Guernsey, one of the United Kingdom's (U.K.) Channel Islands, where he was working post-completion of his residency. In August 2000, we migrated from the U.K. to Canada when my husband obtained a job offer as a physician. So we made the big move from Guernsey to Saskatoon, Saskatchewan. That is when I started leading through service, a path that has shaped me into who I am today.

Career Path: Unlearning and Re-learning

When we arrived in Saskatoon, my husband continued with his work. Meanwhile, I tried to 'get my feet in the workforce' with the possibility of practicing Law. I requested that my law degree results from Nigeria be sent to the National Committee on Accreditation in Ottawa. I wanted to get some advice on how to proceed. When the result came back, I remember reading, "the candidate will be required to complete three years of courses in any Canadian Law school." In hindsight, this was a 'nice' way to tell me to go back to university and study law again. I was not surprised because my results from Nigeria were not top marks and that always played at the back of my mind.

The application and selection process was another thing to contend with—there are only a certain number of spaces and many applicants—the selection is tight. Then there is the Law School Admission Test

---

or state run.

(LSAT) that all potential law school applicants must take. The exam stretched my patience and my resilience. As I pushed on, trying not to be left behind, a friend advised me to apply for any undergraduate program and then apply to law school. That, for me, was a big blow because, for the first time, I felt I was not good enough and had to repeat something. I was used to delays, but never a repeat. That crushed me!

However, I accepted the situation because not redoing the undergraduate degree meant I had to remain where I was when others were moving on with their lives. The best advice I received was to redo my degree since my results from Nigeria could not get me into the Law program. So I reapplied and got accepted into the College of Arts and Science at the University of Saskatchewan, where I studied International Studies. At this point, I had two young children aged three years and six months, respectively. Anyone who has gone through school as a mother knows how stressful it can be to juggle those roles and responsibilities.

These days I laugh when I remember the experiences that made me cry back then. Among the many glimpses I remember from that period of my life is carrying my second son in a baby carrier while doing an online quiz or working through course papers. Toward the end of my degree, I got pregnant with my third child, which was a total surprise! Finishing my final semester was challenging due to some pregnancy-related sickness. I had to push through and use self-motivation not to allow myself the option of quitting or holding off school until my baby was born. This 'no option of quitting' mindset is what I often see among immigrant people, especially those who are highly educated.

The school experience turned out to be enjoyable. I volunteered and served in various leadership roles in a student organisation (Nigerian Association). Whenever I volunteered, I noticed how helping others brought out the best in me. Most of the times I served, I did so because I saw an opportunity to be part of something which revealed itself to serve as part of a bigger purpose. Somebody told me that I was good at spotting opportunities, and they called me spontaneous. I remember 'laughing' that off, not liking being called 'spontaneous' because I didn't see that as a great trait. I will come back to this topic later in the story.

Soon after graduation, in April 2009, my last son was born. Late in 2010, I decided it was time to look for work. However, that took the backburner when my husband informed me that he was due for a sabbatical in July 2011. Sabbatical is a period of paid leave granted to a university teacher or other worker for study or travel, traditionally one year every seven years. At the University of Saskatchewan, it is after six years. Sometimes it could be shorter too, where one can take a six-month sabbatical after three years. My plans had to change, and I had to quickly decide if I wanted to be left alone with three young boys in Saskatoon or go with my husband to Cardiff, Wales, U.K. After that, I had to think about what I would spend my time doing while there.

Going back to school was my best option, given that the U.K. had a recession and the labour market was bleak. I applied for a master's program and was accepted at the University of Glamorgan in Pontypridd, Wales (the university is now called the University of South Wales after merging with another smaller university in Newport, Wales). I studied Human Resources Management, and my final dissertation (or business report as it is referred to) focused on the experiences of foreign doctors within the system and how they were treated. A year after our return to Canada from Wales, my husband and I purchased a clinic, and I started working there as an administrator—but more on that later. I am a lifelong learner and am currently taking an online certificate program in Human Resources Management from Saskatchewan Polytechnic. I started this latest program in August 2021. This course will allow me to fully get into the labour market by opening other opportunities as I transition from my current role at the clinic into my chosen field of human resources.

Leading Despite Mental Illness

As I mentioned earlier, I used to 'laugh' off at being called spontaneous. This is because at age forty, I was diagnosed with Attention Deficit Hyperactivity Disorder (ADHD)[2] and I knew all too well how everything that fell under the umbrella of mental health came with a stigma, especially among my Nigerian community. I must note that not all Nigerians stigmatize those with mental illnesses, but there is a general lack of awareness of the mental illness, and learning disabilities are often viewed through a very narrow lens. So, being referred to as spontaneous was a huge burden that I didn't want to carry.

My spontaneity made me 'loud.' The constant joke was: "You always know Halima is around because you hear her voice before you see her." For those of us with ADHD, there is impulsivity—and although I have never been on an impulse major shopping spree, several little things got me into trouble! Being loud and impulsive meant that most things I commented on somehow missed the filtering, and my mouth spoke faster than my brain. For example, a common issue was that whenever I saw someone struggling with anything, I stepped in to pray with them, even if we were in a public space. I could not let the need pass, especially if I could do something such as offer a simple prayer.

Indeed, soon after we moved to Canada, we found a church and made it our home church. One day I remember how fast I offered my help when, during service, it was announced that someone was needed to help with teaching the older children. I always showed up, and someone told me that I had a way with the babies and toddlers. I was eventually asked to

---

2. A very brief description of ADHD- it is a brain disorder with three main features-inattention, hyperactivity, and impulsivity. Some people may have one of the above listed features or a combination of the three features (https://www.betterhelp.com). To write about ADHD is honestly a book for another day and not something that can be condensed into a book chapter that is focused on a different topic. A book chapter is not going to be enough to do justice to the topic of ADHD. At the very least, if you do notice any of the three symptoms, it is wise and important to seek help from a physician or a trained counsellor that specializes in mental health. There will be links at the end of the book with helpful links with useful information about ADHD.

help coordinate that side of Children's Ministry. I covered this role from 2003 to 2004. I then moved on to serve in my church board of elders or spiritual care team from 2005 to this day. Serving on the board included hospital visits if people were admitted and home visits for those who wanted the elders to come to their home to pray together. As elders, most times, we even prayed with church members that wanted prayers during worship. I always tried to remember the faces of the people I prayed with to check with them how things were going on. It takes a certain level of confidence to walk up to a stranger and ask how they are doing by reminding them that you prayed with them earlier.

When the Women's Ministry was growing, we always had events in the spring, fall, and summer. We would have summer Bible studies and talks by different people and experts. I was surprised when the organizers asked me to help with ticket sales. The women's pastor said: "Halima, you have a natural gift of hospitality. Could you be in charge of ticket sales for this event?" That led to many more seasons taking the lead with ticket sales. I had to collaborate with people—knowing those who were comfortable speaking to people or would rather be at the desk dealing with cash transactions while I did the talking. Sometimes I would show up early and say: "Ladies, I thought I'd come in early to help you out. What can I do to help? Put me to use."

Having a 'disorder' did not stop me from thriving; it may have come at a cost, but it has turned out to be a blessing that others can benefit from. It has also taught me that 'spontaneity' can be channeled by practicing mindfulness. Also, walking has been beneficial because it allows me to slow down my active mind.

Opening a Clinic Practice

One of my memorable 'spontaneous' thinking moments happened in early 2013. One of my husband's colleagues in the private sector wanted to sell her clinic because she was moving to British Columbia. When my husband told me about the sale, I encouraged him to go for it and buy the place. He was reluctant to do so because someone had already made an offer. When we heard that it was unsuccessful, I told my husband to try to make an offer again. He did in August of that year we got the place. Then came the task of setting up a practice. We had to ask experienced people to help us. That required humility because we needed to learn about the requirements to open a clinic in Saskatoon. There was so much work that went into it. The learning curve was steep! There was so much sacrifice before things started moving. That was humbling, AARRGHH!

I had to learn how to deal with different people with different temperaments, biases, and, sometimes, prejudiced behaviours. Some were assets for sure, while some taught me life lessons. However, there was, and there is still no way, that one runs a business or leads without realizing that the workers, partners, and, most importantly, patients must come first. And in clinical practice, an authoritative leadership style must be at the bottom, while serving the needs of staff, colleagues, and patients must be at the top.

The clinic practice became operational in May 2014. I wish I could say it was all fun and hitch-free. Unfortunately, anything that could go wrong went wrong. First, a poor connection with the fax resulted in faxed requests not going through or coming through late. The medical EMR was spotty because of the poor internet connection, and there was still so much to learn with staff payroll. And then the paperwork with Canada Revenue Agency (CRA), how to file GST and make remittances that I had no clue about as we were starting—in other words, we were fledgling. Fortunately, we overcame these challenges and others as they came up. Because of all the mistakes, the CRA audited us often, so we learned. The best teacher is always the mistakes and challenges we face and how we deal with them.

It is 2022 now, and although, like most businesses, the COVID-19 pandemic affected us, we are still operating. We had to make some tough decisions. Nowadays, I maintain elementary work at the clinic. Among the many lessons I learned from starting and running my own business (with my husband), one I hold dear is humility. I accept correction from people who have the experience to correct my mistakes or give good advice. I fondly remember my father's advice when starting this clinic practice: "Never go a pay period without paying your staff." I have always ensured that I pay my staff in a timely fashion. I also learned to be of service—checking up on the team and getting them little thank-you gifts, leaving them little snacks, or simply making them coffee. Offering a personable approach and proactively appreciating my staff have contributed to some stability in recruitment and retention because most staff members have stayed with us.

A Life Story and Leadership Lessons

When I reflect on my life experiences, I recognize that one must be humble when learning from well-meaning people who have been through similar experiences before. However, the humility in constantly learning has kept me going in my leadership of others by holding their hands and being their cheerleader. Servant leadership has come from my life experiences and my faith. Faith is vital in my life, and it has guided me to be a servant to people.

People tell their stories because storytelling is universal, and stories give voices to the voiceless. Telling our story can make readers relate and not feel alone in their struggles. Storytelling is a way to build connections and understanding while teaching, encouraging, and influencing others. May my story resonates with those whose paths are less conventional. I hope it challenges people to think deeper and broader about leadership.

I've also learned that one must learn to lead thyself before leading others. Take the challenges and hurdles presented on your way in stride and put one foot in front of the other to keep moving. As you put that foot in front of the other, know that others have been there and have made a path for you to go on. Where there is no path, be vulnerable to serve and create your way for others to follow.

"

THE TRUE HEROES OF THE NEW MILLENNIUM WILL BE SERVANT LEADERS, QUIETLY WORKING OUT OF THE SPOTLIGHT TO TRANSFORM OUR WORLD.

— Ann McGee-Cooper

Meet The Author

Portia Sarah Manzini was born and raised in South Africa. She received her Bachelor of Jurisprudence and Bachelor of Laws from University of the North, South Africa.

She is passionate about community development, and has worked as a Skills Development facilitator and trainer, to empower women and the community at large to make them aware of their rights and ability to change the world.

As a devoted Philanthropist, she founded Count Blessings Outreach in 2019 and her greatest efforts are dedicated to developing projects to empower Women and Girls living in rural areas.

Her love for healthy community living and family relations drove her to spend her Friday evenings in the streets of Saskatoon serving in the Bus street "ministry of love and hope" encouraging and reminding the homeless that GOD loves them and as His servant she is here to offer support.

She loves writing and some of her stories have been published in Obaahima: *Kingdom Woman* journal. She has also written a devotional book *A Victorious Life*.

She lives in Saskatoon with her husband and three children.

Portia Sarah Manzini

"

TAKE CONTROL OF YOUR MIND
BEFORE IT TAKES CONTROL OF YOU.

– P. S. Manzini

Chapter 7

THE CHALLENGE OF BECOMING

by Portia Sarah Manzini

Change is a challenge that needs to be challenged.
– P. S. Manzini

Ding-dong
"Cabin crew, prepare for landing. Ladies and gentlemen, welcome to Saskatoon. It's a beautiful warm day; the temperature is eighteen degrees Celsius. We wish you a wonderful stay."
Ding-dong.

Reality hit me when I heard the captain's announcement. After six months apart, I was finally meeting my husband, Prince Charming. The journey had been long, across the Atlantic from South Africa, with only a handbag for myself and my three little children. This trip was my first overseas journey to an unknown place, so initially, I decided to pack everything I could and ended up with eight huge suitcases that could have fitted a minivan. Sadly, I had to bring seven bags with none of my clothing. I had to prioritize the children's needs and get their items.

My youngest son was fast asleep due to the considerable time difference. The only solution was to drag him out of his seat and make my way out of the plane. I was grateful when another mother helped me put my thirty pounds little one on my back so he could continue to sleep.

What a beautiful moment for a family to reunite and start a new life together. Though a bit disoriented, I was excited to finally realize my dream of living on the other side of the world, Canada, a place I used to admire, thanks to National Geographic Channel and Cartoons Network shows.

Leaving my comfort zone and familiar territories was a huge step and a challenge, but determination made me leap. As a leader, I embrace stepping out of my comfort zone; it is one of the qualities that makes a person stand out and make a difference in their life, community, and the world.

I am a trailblazer. The first in my family to take this huge step of moving abroad. When we arrived, the voice of fear saying, "You are all alone with no family support or friends in Canada," started singing in my head for a long time. If I had danced to that music, I would have taken the next flight back to South Africa.

Instead, I reminded myself that I could do everything through Christ, who strengthens me. If you want to see change, don't wait for someone, but start creating a path for that change. There are lots of opportunities that avail themselves to all of us in different ways and times. Some will realize it and grab it, and some will miss it. Many factors can contribute to missing out. It can be ignorance, fear of the unknown, cultural practices, etc. I saw an opportunity to come to Saskatchewan, Canada, and I grabbed it.

However, I had to give up some important things along the way. I was about to celebrate my LLB graduation in South Africa, but to not lose my flight ticket to Canada for the second time, I gave that up and graduated in absentia. I was still happy, though, because I thought I would be able to do my bar examination and become an attorney in Saskatchewan. This was an opportunity not to be missed, to become that attorney I have always wanted to become. However, that part of the journey was less smooth sailing than I had thought. I needed help to have my South African qualifications recognized by the Canadian system. Nevertheless, I silently continued to encourage myself, saying, "Portia, get up and go; this is the time to break barriers, shatter ceilings, move every obstacle, change the narrative, come against all odds, and have a story that will shape your best future and live with no regrets."

Leaping over Barriers and Walls

Martin Luther King said, "I have a dream". This is the undeniable truth. We all have dreams. My dream was to become a Family Advocate and a voice for the oppressed. I remember that my father used to ask me one question repeatedly: "What do you want to be when you grow up?" I always gave him the same answer: "I want to be a lawyer." He encouraged me every Sunday by giving me a comic page from the Sunday newspaper. I could see myself just like the judge in that cartoon, with funny hair and glasses almost falling off his face.

Coming to Canada created more opportunities for me, being in another country, speaking a different language and learning new skills. This was the time to turn my shelved dream into reality. I was ready to dive into the pool of opportunities this country had to offer. I polished my resume, did my best to get myself out there, and knocked on different doors. Some opened, and others slammed at my face, but I kept going. I was disappointed and heartbroken along the journey, but I never allowed a negative mindset to hinder my mission. On paper, I had all the right skills to land a job, but due to different perceptions, doors that were wide open closed for me.

I still speak with an accent because I am multilingual. In South Africa, I would be a top employee because I can speak at least six of my official native languages. My determination kept me going. I asked myself this million-dollar question: "Why is the door always shutting?" I realized that the one behind the door didn't want my accent, and the high qualifications posed a threat to their business. I'm still on a mission to make my dream of becoming an attorney come, even though sometimes I don't understand what is expected from me.

In life, at times, you will not understand what is expected from you to realize your dream. All you can do as a dream chaser is to move forward and focus on what is ahead of you instead of the roadblock.

Perseverance is key to success. Quitters always lose. I am not one, and I do not encourage anyone to be one. Never lose hope; instead, change your approach, and discover more opportunities. When one door closes, ten more doors will open, with wider choices. Sometimes when you come across a wall and a barrier, the thing that's holding you back is in your mind.

> If you cannot go around it, leap over and get a safe landing
> – P. S. Manzini

When Cultures Collide

> In Africa, we have a concept known as Ubuntu—the profound sense that we are human only through the humanity of others; that if we are to accomplish anything in this world it will in equal measure be due to the work and achievement of others
> – Nelson Mandela

Our cultural background contributes to the way we live our everyday life. Our comfort makes us resist change.

As a child, I remember playing around my neighbourhood's dusty streets with homemade toys from every scrap I could find. I was always excited for the weekend because I knew that, from morning until evening, I was going to play with almost every child in the neighbourhood. Saying hello to everyone who passed by was my favourite, and if they acknowledged me with a smile, that was more precious than gold. All these practices cultivated in me the love for always having company.

When I arrived in Canada, I expected the same. One weekend I opened the door hoping to say hello to someone passing by the street. Instead, there was no sign of life, only sadness, and disappointment. Suddenly, everything had to be recreated—new friends, neighbours, and other relationships. Alone without much guidance, I asked myself: "Where and how do I start? Do I say hello to strangers and expect a smile back?" I was in for an adventure. Half of the population in the small town of Nipawin had never seen Black people at a close range. I gave it a second thought. "What was I thinking coming to this place?"

However, the welcome baskets from my neighbours, which filled my kitchen floor with all kinds of snacks, made me think: "There is still hope to start all over." I immediately adjusted my mindset and reminded myself that I was in a land where the people had a different culture than my own. My mind started to welcome other options for information and new relations. I was ready to share my adventure and hoped people would share theirs too.

The next day I peeked through the window, thinking I would see someone passing by, but instead, the streets were empty as a midnight train. I had never seen anything like that in my life. "Maybe it was still early, and someone will pass by later." I thought to myself, peeking through the window for many days, only to see two people passing by my street with a dog on a leash. "Is this real, or do I imagine things?" I asked myself this question for at least three months, only to find out it was the norm. This was not the crowded street, full of giggles, dogs running loose and enjoying their free time kind of place.

There were many other culture shocks: cars driving on the right side of the road, and you don't say hello to anyone unless you know them, you don't go to someone's house unless they invite you, you are not automatically part of the dinner table unless you are invited for dinner. When someone invited you to eat out, you had to pay for your own meal because this is how the locals roll. Youngsters are comfortable calling elders by their names. I thought I was losing my mind. Wow! This collision was about to explode.

One immigrant lady who arrived earlier in the community invited me to a local church one Sunday. After the service, she introduced me to a few ladies. When I respond to one of them saying: "So, you are sister Helen!" She quickly corrected me, saying: "No, call me Helen. When you say sister, it is not right; we are not siblings." In my culture, you say sister to someone as a sign of respect and care. But the reality is that we are shaped by different cultures and practices, which are all beautiful in the eyes of the beholder. From that moment onwards, I continually tried to know the major cultural differences and started to enjoy my new relations.

When my culture is different from my neighbour's culture, it doesn't mean that their culture is right or better than mine. Also, I have learned that I don't have to change how I was brought up or adopt other people's ways to fit in or vice versa. Instead, we can acknowledge each other and work together with our diverse cultural backgrounds with respect and love. This is an opportunity to explore and learn from one another.

Embrace your Learning Journey

Once, I was humbled by a mother who had adopted a Black child. She came to ask me for advice on how she could take care of her child's hair. I really appreciated that. I gave her thumbs up for being a brave woman and for helping a child who was victimized by the circumstances and ended up as an orphan. What an opportunity I had been given.

"Can I touch your hair?" she asked.

"Of course," I responded. She was so excited to finally meet someone who knew about afro hair, the information she needed to make a difference in an innocent child's life. I made sure that the next day when we met at the parking lot to pick up our kids after school, I brought my whole hair products for her to take home and try. This act fulfilled my day and encouraged me to continue to give attention and time to those willing to learn new things.

Speaking of learning, one pivotal moment in my leadership journey happened back home in South Africa. Our government hired me as a Skills Training Specialist to lead a group of rural women in South Africa to own and manage a bush lodge, similar to a cabin accommodation out in the woods.

The project involved a group of women with different education levels, with only one who had completed grade twelve. My role was to teach the basic principles of business. Most of these women could only speak their mother tongue and hardly spoke English. I had to design the study materials to accommodate their literacy levels. Sometimes, I used interpreters to help the women understand the lessons. This process took a lot of patience as I was determined to ensure that the women felt comfortable being in class and learning business skills. I noticed some women were embarrassed because they could not Speak English. I just encouraged them to keep going. This training took about six months; in the end, all the women had their banking accounts. One highlight of this project I'm still proud was seeing a 70-year-old woman learn to use a calculator, read, and complete a bank deposit slip. I considered this a huge success for the project.

This leadership experience taught me not to undermine people based on their age, background, or education level. Anybody can learn with determination. I also learned to manage and resolve conflict immediately among the group members; due to different personality dynamics, sometimes conflict would arise. I was able to listen to and resolve challenging issues within the team to maintain a cohesive team environment. This project's success has proven that anything is possible when a leader is positive. Later, when I drove past this place, other ideas about empowering women emerged. I believe that if we want to see our communities grow, as women, we need to take on leadership roles.

Also in Canada, I started enjoying my prairie life. I met one kind friend, Betty, from a neighbourhood church. One day she took me to Wapiti Ski resort. That was a moment for me to discover my skiing hidden talent—on the bunny hill. I fell like rotten fruit from a tree multiple time. However, I encouraged and amazed at the compliments I got from everyone, even small kids saying "Don't worry you will get it, we all started there, you are brave." Eleanor Roosevelt, former First Lady of the United States, said "Great leaders inspires people to have confidence in themselves." Those people that cheered me on , that day, inspired me to have confidence in myself. I considered them as great leaders. That experience also taught me to hope for the best everyday.

Another example of how I embraced my learning journey was when, out of curiosity, I asked a program officers if she could take me to the countryside. She was welcoming, and I saw that she was willing to introduce me to the Canadian lifestyle. Little did I know that she was just waiting for the moment I would ask her. What an adventure to fulfill my dream: ride a horse, go to a chuckwagon race, roast marshmallows, and make smores. That was one of the most memorable adventures of my life. Thanks to Jessie, I got inspired to do more activities like fishing and camping. Life in the prairies was becoming real and enjoyable. I kept hoping for the best every day.

People perish because they lack knowledge. To be ignorant is dangerous. There are two types of people in this world. The ignorant and the ones who lack knowledge. The ignorant deliberately commit a certain act, but the ones who lack knowledge don't get an opportunity to learn. Whenever I met people that lacked knowledge, if they asked me what kind of tan I use for my skin, I allowed them to rub my arm and prove it was indeed my natural skin. I was amazed by their appreciation of my skin tone. As for the more ignorant ones, I decided to stand firm and leave no room for any form of discrimination, with the hope and anticipation that at a later stage, when they acquired proper information and understood things better, they would treat all human beings equally, with respect and dignity.

Wherever you go, you will experience some form of unacceptable treatment by a fellow human. It is not one size fits all. There are still some good potatoes in a whole bag of rotten ones. Choose the good ones and throw the bad ones before they contaminate the whole bag. Do not miss opportunities because of ignorant people who refuse to adjust to change; instead, grab those opportunities and use them to teach the ignorant. Use every platform to bring a message of change, hope and love instead of promoting hatred and undermining other minds because of their outside look. We are created differently by God, we look different outside, but the same inside. We have the same abilities and capabilities. Any human-being can acquire a skill and is able to make a difference in this world. You are human, so you are capable.

Positive and Negative Mindset in one Container

With all the hurdles I had to jump as high as possible, I chose to be positive and give people the benefit of the doubt. No two people are the same. I chose to focus on the positive people who were willing to learn more about my roots and my culture, people who saw their dream coming true by getting to know me. As much as they were inquisitive and curious like cats, it was also important for me to know their culture as part of my new way of life. In fact, with this attitude, I took an opportunity to become a Care Group Leader in my church. Every Wednesday, I met and had fellowship with my group members. We learned from each other's cultures by sharing our favourite recipes. We also shared both joys and life struggles. My role was to listen and understand them and be able to make sure their needs were met. Most of the team members were older than me, as they were now in their senior years.

This leadership experience taught me how to interact and connect with seniors. I appreciate the time I spent with my group members. I had to make sure I spent time developing trust and maintaining confidentiality, as sometimes we discussed sensitive matters. Apart from the age factor, I had to deal with cultural differences as I was from Africa, and most of them were born and grew up here as Canadians. I was open to learning more about their culture as they learned about mine. As a leader, I learned humility and respect when working with others, particularly when they are different from me. These are lessons I carry with me everywhere.

I realized that your life is influenced by two mindsets: positive and negative. These two are always fighting each other, either one with a desire to win. The responsibility of which mindset wins rests upon you. You are challenged to choose which voice to listen to in your everyday life. The world is full of both negative and positive people. As a leader, you are tried and tested by both. When you allow negativity to dominate your atmosphere, you will become a loser, and when positivity dominates your atmosphere, you become a winner. This world needs strong, positive leaders who desire to make a difference in people's lives and the environment. It only takes a positive mindset to achieve this.

The Lessons

To grow and impact others, a leader responds to a challenging and painful change with a positive and hopeful attitude. You are a leader once you get hold of opportunities and use them positively. Leading by example requires a lot of effort and determination. Leadership is not completed by only acquiring a specific title because leaders need to act and practice what they preach. They can have a certificate or training in leadership, but if they don't positively impact others with their learned skills, they have not proven they can lead. They say action speaks louder than words. Many people are inactive in their leadership positions. In short, a leader must put into practice the knowledge they acquire. Their ability must be tested.

Leading will not come easy. It involves a combination of skills and approaches. One must have relevant tools to begin the process of leadership. I take it as an aging process. Your endurance and ability to solve problems, impart knowledge, transfer skills of empowerment, advocating for others whose voices are silenced. People must see hope for a better world when they meet you.

Winning leaders have a positive mindset from the beginning of a challenge. They view a challenge as an opportunity to be creative and test their ability and thought process. We are all born with the possibility and ability to do great things. Your willing mind will make that possible. No one is born a leader, but everyone can become a leader. Are you ready to make a change in your life and in the life of the people around you? Are you prepared to be that trailblazer leader?

NO ONE IS BORN HATING ANOTHER PERSON BECAUSE OF THE COLOUR OF HIS SKIN, OR HIS BACKGROUND, OR HIS RELIGION. PEOPLE MUST LEARN TO HATE AND IF THEY CAN LEARN TO HATE, THEY CAN BE TAUGHT TO LOVE

– Nelson Mandela

Meet The Author

Theodocia Quagraine is a proud Ghanaian-Canadian woman residing in Saskatoon, Treaty Six Territory, land of the Metis. By trade, she works in the tech industry but her passion lies in being a connector and mentorship.

Her passion led her to become a co-founder/director of BIPOC Coffee Talk Inc. and become involved in multiple non-profits aimed to empower and help people.

Her memoir in this book features her experiences with bullying, struggling with low self-worth, and transforming into the leader she is today. She hopes to inspire young Black girls to chase their dreams despite any obstacles.

Theodocia Quagraine

INSTEAD OF LETTING YOUR HARDSHIPS AND FAILURES DISCOURAGE OR EXHAUST YOU, LET THEM INSPIRE YOU. LET THEM MAKE YOU EVEN HUNGRIER TO SUCCEED."

- Michelle Obama

Chapter 8

RISING ABOVE DOUBT

by Theodocia Quagraine

I smiled and waved at my laptop screen as I gave my final farewell to the CBC interviewer. My dining room, which earlier was echoing with the sound of voices while my business partner and I described to the CBC interviewer the discussion-based club we had created two months prior, was now quiet. I took my headphones off and dazedly stared around my small dining room with a face full of make-up, wearing a formal shirt, and pajama bottoms, which had become my custom attire since the early months of the 2020 pandemic. I sat in silence, reflecting on the video interview that had just occurred and the impact it had on me. At the end of the call, we were told that the interview would air on all CBC Saskatchewan outlets. I was filled with pride at this enormous personal achievement. I know a video interview isn't as monumental of achievement to certain folks as it was for me, and I'm sure many people skimmed past the video to see the new COVID-19 updates when it was posted. But for me, that interview was a big deal. It showed me the progress I had made throughout the years and the struggles I had overcome to get to a point when I was confident enough to complete that video interview. As I was sitting silently in my dining room, I was reminded of my younger self, the one who lacked confidence and frequently stayed silent because she believed no one cared about what she had to say. More specifically, I was reminded of my pre-teen years.

Younger Self

I was born in Ghana, and when I was four years old, my family immigrated to Canada, settling in Saskatchewan. I grew up in a family of six: my father, mother, older brother, twin sister, and little sister. My siblings and I are close in age. I remember going on many bike adventures during the weekends. I had an innocent goofiness with my family and close friends. I was also inquisitive and creative. As a pre-teen, I was tall and slender, wore glasses, and my hair was often in braids. My head has always been full of creative ideas that yearned to come to life, and I'm grateful that I was allowed to express them. I enjoyed creating cartoons, sewing, editing, video and photography, and painting. I was ecstatic when my parents bought me pastels, paint, sewing kits, and other tools to express my creativity. I was noticeably quiet and shy in school and found it difficult to maintain eye contact. Though my school was more diverse than most Saskatchewan public schools at the time, I was still one of the few African-descent kids. Many students were the children of international students, including myself. One of my fondest memories from those years was learning about many cultures and religions in our school and developing an appreciation for multiculturalism, a value I still hold today.

I have always had a gentle and calming spirit. I went with the flow and got along with most folks. I was raised to be courteous and respectful. I would often thank people after they helped me. I was quick to apologize when I offended someone. Showing respect was a moral value instilled in me at an early age, to the point that I did it reflexively. I believed that if I treated others with respect, they would do the same with me. I thought that if someone treated you poorly, they were upset with something you did.

Unfortunately, I learned in my younger years that there are people out there who aren't going to like you for being your authentic self. I learned this lesson in fourth grade when a boy in my class bullied me. I'm amazed that I still remember in which grade it happened—that's how much it impacted me. I can't recall exactly how it started or why he targeted me.

He wasn't someone I noticed before the bullying, and I don't remember any interactions with him beforehand. My first memory of him is when he attempted to trip me over as I walked to pick up an item from a shelf near his desk. That first incident led to many other random juvenile incidents and slowly started to involve more peers.

The bullying included making fun of my full name and appearance, pointing out that I didn't wear designer clothes, and accusing me of stealing.

At times it got physical. One day, during recess, one boy ripped off my jacket and threw it on the ground. I was so confused; I didn't know what I had done wrong that triggered that kind of treatment. Mentally, I went through all my interactions with these people and tried to figure out what I did that led them to treat me disrespectfully, but I couldn't think of anything. I just wanted it to stop! Coincidentally, many bullying campaigns were going on during this time. The consistent message in all of them was to tell an adult, whether it was a parent or teacher. Seeing these campaigns gave me hope; I felt like I had finally found the solution to ease the pain I was experiencing. I first told my parents and eventually said a teacher.

My parents took my assertion seriously, but the teachers failed me. I felt like they didn't take me seriously. They didn't do enough to prevent the escalated bullying that occurred afterward. The physical incidents I mentioned above occurred after I informed the teachers that I was being bullied. Some of their poor judgment included, for example, a teacher leaving me alone in the hallway with the bully. Once the teacher left, the bully started taunting me, calling me names for getting him in trouble. Being put in the hallway with my bully felt like I was also being punished, even though I was the victim. Another incident was the bully throwing a soft toy at my face after I had dropped it near him. When I told my teacher, who was close by when it happened, they responded that the toy was soft and didn't hurt. My issue wasn't whether it caused physical pain or not. My point was that someone shouldn't be so disrespectful that they would throw an item at someone.

I felt so invalidated by those teachers that I stopped reporting future events. I didn't see the point of doing so anymore; I felt nothing would change if I told them. It was just getting worse. I felt so powerless. Writing these pages, this memoir, is a tremendously emotional journey for me. I've had to relive hurtful moments like these. I didn't realize how much these negative memories impacted me. The bullying I experienced made me have low self-esteem, making me believe that my voice didn't matter. The light of the goofy and inquisitive girl, with a head full of ideas, within me dimmed. It remained darkened until the end of high school.

The dimmed version of myself remained until a life-changing moment. In high school, I heard that a girl from my old elementary school had died by suicide from being relentlessly bullied for a long time. I remembered her; she was lovely, eccentric, and always had a smile. I remember chatting with her occasionally when I walked home from school because we lived in the same neighbourhood. The news of her death hit me hard. I was familiar with that hopeless feeling that may have led her to make that irreversible decision. Even now, it deeply hurts me when I hear stories about bullying and discrimination. These painful incidents in my life didn't break me. Instead, they motivated me to aim to become the mentor I needed. Someone who would listen, validate, reaffirm, and instill confidence in the youth around her. This motivation led me to start many initiatives and participate in countless others. I desired to protect vulnerable people and let them know that life gets better. I wanted to be a living example—life did get better for me. My light started returning; I finally found my life's purpose.

Becoming a Leader

Elementary school and high school passed. During my years in university my interest in becoming a leader started to bloom. Before that time, I did not peg myself as the "leader type." I viewed great leaders as influential, charismatic, assertive, and wise, which were traits I didn't believe I possessed. However, my perspective and ability to see me as a leader changed in my final year of university. During a group assignment, I volunteered to be the art director for a project-based digital culture and new media class. We were tasked to create a website that told a story about an element of Saskatoon. Our group picked the Broadway neighbourhood, one of the oldest neighbourhoods in Saskatoon with a rich history. As the art director, I managed the development and design team. Simply put, I led the folks who coded the website and those who created the graphics for the website. I was familiar with both web development and design aspects, so I accepted the challenge.

I am not assertive, but when I believe there is a lack of organisation or direction within a group, I find myself stepping in to establish order. Now, with my knowledge of all the different leadership styles, I recognize that I was using a coaching leadership style. I set up one-on-one meetings with my team members to see how they were doing and if they needed any help. I delegated roles that they wanted and would enjoy. I also helped a team member who wanted to learn how to code. Not to sound conceited, but I did excellent in that role. I was knowledgeable in the area I was leading, which made me comfortable, yet I was also humble enough to know that my team members were also knowledgeable, and we all learned a lot from each other. It didn't feel like there was a hierarchy, just peers collaborating to create an interactive website for our final project.

As a leader, I acted as a project manager to ensure we met our deadlines, and beyond that, we were equal. It was a fantastic experience, and I was very appreciative when we received anonymous feedback from our teammates. I received many positive comments. That experience solidified in me that I had what it takes to become a good leader. I influenced the group with my thoughts for the project, I was charismatic by staying optimistic despite any obstacles we faced, I was assertive when I needed to be, and I was knowledgeable about the topic and desired to learn more. Once the project was over and the hectic university schedule had ended, I had time to reflect. I recognized that I had a confidence problem that stemmed from being bullied, and I often second-guessed myself. This mindset was holding me back from many things I wanted to accomplish. After the university ended, I sought counseling to address this problem.

Internal Confidence

If you were to ask my family, friends, co-workers, and anyone who has spent significant time with me how to describe me, I'm sure the word that would come up the most is quiet. That was the recurring comment in my report cards. I realized that being labeled as 'quiet' was not seen as positive. It was often accompanied by efforts to 'break me out of my shell.' I perceived the quiet label as a negative trait that needed to be changed. This subtle label, being bullied in grade school, and not feeling validated or heard led to deep insecurities that have had lasting effects. This self-doubt puts me in a negative cycle that starts with me keeping my thoughts to myself. I don't feel heard when I speak, so I stay quiet, which leads to my thoughts not being known. I wanted to break this cycle, but figuring out where to start was overwhelming, and I needed help. I sought a counselor and started my mental health journey. The first couple of sessions were rough; I found it exceedingly difficult to be vulnerable and found myself underplaying the depression I felt.

I eventually opened up to a counselor and I felt comfortable. It was uplifting to share an experience that upset me and get feedback on it with empathy and understanding. When I was vulnerable in the past, I felt dismissed or made to feel like I was being too sensitive. But in counseling, I was asked questions that revealed the thought I created behind an action, thoughts that usually centered around the theme of low self-worth. Those thoughts were then challenged and replaced with more helpful ideas, which was a massive improvement from what I was used to. Through years of counseling, I've learned how to be vulnerable with people by identifying and expressing my feelings. Learning to accept the 'quiet and sensitive' label I'm often given is still challenging, but I recognize that those traits also contribute to my good leadership skills. For example, I'm detail oriented, a good listener, and have a good memory, which are traits attributed to people with quiet and sensitive temperament. I choose to recognize and celebrate all my progress, big or small, and counseling has helped me build the confidence I needed to step out of my comfort zone.

Toastmasters

A moment I stepped way out of my comfort zone was when I decided to join a club called Toastmasters. When I started my first full-time job after university, I found out that I had to speak in groups and had to deliver numerous presentations that year. I was terrified and getting incredibly nervous. When I told an acquaintance I wanted to improve my public speaking, they mentioned Toastmasters. This is an international organisation that consists of many clubs that aim to build your leadership and communication skills. I had heard about that organisation many years prior. As soon as I listened to a Toastmasters on campus, and they were hosting an open house, I decided to check it out. I enjoyed the first meeting. It was nerve-wracking but still enjoyable. After that, I didn't join the campus Toastmasters club, but I eventually joined another club years later.

Every club is different; some are more professional and run like a political office. Others, like the club I ended up joining, are more casual and have a family feel. Each club meeting consists of activities to help members practice impromptu speaking, evaluating, and running a punctual meeting. I didn't feel comfortable participating in the beginning, but with the encouragement of my club members, I stepped out of my comfort zone and challenged myself to reach milestones I didn't think were possible. For example, one milestone I achieved was winning the best table topics. Table topics is an impromptu speaking game where an individual is asked a random question and is given two minutes to answer. It seemed simple enough. However, I dreaded attending for the first couple of years because I was terrible at table topics. I would get so nervous that I would blank. I would usually stand in silence for what felt like hours while trying to find an answer. Then, after many minutes of awkward looks, I would start rambling and saying things that seemed jumbled and nonsensical while using numerous filler words like "uh" and "um." I would feel so embarrassed afterward that sometimes I couldn't bring myself back the following week.

I feared my club members thought I was dumb and that they hated hearing my attempt at impromptu speaking. I felt ashamed because it seemed so easy for the other members. I did get better, so I searched for techniques I could use to improve my improvisational skills. I found a speaking template online that I followed to organize my thoughts. That helped my response become clear and organized. I used pauses and talked slower instead of using filler words. I accepted that there wasn't a correct or best answer and spoke about whatever came to my mind first. I used stories to explain my response, and I became better at public speaking. When I won best table topics for the first time, I felt so proud. My hard work had paid off, and I was improving; people noticed. I accepted that communication, like many other things in life, is a skill anyone can improve. With this newly found skill and confidence under my belt, I wanted to use them outside the toastmasters' walls.

Starting a Business

One day, in the summer of 2020, I was spending time with a friend doing crafts when the topic of race and dating came up. We are both women of colour in a 'white' city. Quietly, I listened to my friend share her experience because being vulnerable was still new. I was surprised to hear how many things she shared to which I could relate. Even though we were not of the same ethnicity and had different life experiences, our feelings were similar. The conversation was friendly, and I yearned to have more conversations where folks could validate each other and stand in solidarity. So, I reached out to her the next day asking if she wanted to start a club for people of colour, where we could have conversations like the one we shared the previous night. I asked her because she had expressed interest in starting a club earlier, and even though I was willing to do it myself, I could see the value in having a business partner. I was happy she agreed! In the next couple of months, we planned our mission statement, created a logo, and opened our social media pages.

In October 2020, we made our first post. I remember that day vividly. It was midnight, we had just finished a long night of working, and we were ready to publish. My stomach sank when we posted for the first time. So many thoughts ran through my mind: "Would folks be offended that we want to create a group for Black, Indigenous, and People of Colour (BIPOC)? Would it lead to hate messages? What if we don't get any engagement, or worse, what if we get engagement and our idea becomes a reality?" We shared our page with a couple of friends and got a good engagement shortly after posting. Wow! The response was so encouraging; seeing folks interested in joining our discussions that it led to a CBC interview shortly after seemed so unreal.

I was shocked to see how many people cared and wanted to learn how to improve the world for people of colour. I was expecting another experience like my early years, where I felt unheard, but I was pleasantly surprised when we got that warm response. Providing a space where folks could vent and feel heard was so rewarding. Learning new ways to support my BIPOC, ally sisters and brothers, was very enriching. The importance of partnership in leadership roles was evident when creating this club—benefiting from the strengths of each individual within the group. For example, my strength is behind-the-scenes work, like organizing, planning, video editing, creating graphics, and starting initiatives.

On the other hand, my business partner's strength was written and verbal communication. The partnership worked because we complimented each other and made up for the areas that weren't our natural strengths. I learned that the beauty of collaboration lies in folks using their unique assets to create something great.

Continue to Learn

One of my core values is personal development, and as I mentioned earlier, one of my life missions is to become the mentor I needed as a child. To answer that longing, I searched for leadership courses that would allow me to become a better leader for the discussion group my business partner and I created. That is when I found the Global Empowerment Initiative for Women Inc. (GEIWI) leadership training for Black women leaders. It was a perfect opportunity for me to develop my leadership skills. The fact that a Black woman was leading it was the icing on the cake. I was intrigued to join the leadership group because I could attend many communication, leadership, and mental health workshops. I knew these workshops were going to help me achieve my goal. My involvement with GEIWI leadership training led me to write this chapter in this collaborative book project. Today, I remain open to new opportunities that may present themselves in the future.

My life experiences have led me to become the person I am today. They have forged my resilience and prompted me to define my self-worth. I've embraced the fact that being quiet is my biggest strength. It strengthens my leadership skills because it allows me to be meticulous, a good listener, and have a good memory. Because I was bullied in grade school, I have become more empathetic. Because the experience was damaging to my mental health, I don't want anyone to go through it; I want to help vulnerable people stand up for themselves. I like to be someone who instills confidence and teaches everyone that they are unconditionally worthy regardless of their success. Toastmasters gave me the confidence to speak in public, and starting a non-profit club taught me that my voice matters. I've identified that my purpose in life is to inspire people to embrace who they are authentically and learn how to use their natural strengths to achieve their goals in life. I've learned that anyone can improve themselves while staying true to their identity. All the experiences we have in life, even if negative, can shape us to become a better version of ourselves if we identify the positive lesson from them and apply it.

Resilience is a theme found in many Black women's stories, and though that's powerful, I hope to see a future in which struggling and being Black aren't interconnected. Everything I do from this point on is done in the hope of seeing Black women not working or handling their burdens on their own. I hope to see a future where, from a young age, Black girls see their unconditional worthiness, know that their voices matter, and are validated and celebrated. Starting BIPOC Coffee Talk Inc., a discussion-based club where folks can share their experiences in solidarity, is my biggest leadership accomplishment to date, and I'm just getting started.

NEVER LIMIT YOURSELF BECAUSE OF OTHERS' LIMITED IMAGINATION; NEVER LIMIT OTHERS BECAUSE OF YOUR OWN LIMITED IMAGINATION.

–Dr. Mae Jemison

Meet The Author

Hannah Ngozi Eby Chukwu, PhD, holds graduate degrees from the University of Nigeria, Nsukka, and the University of Saskatchewan, Saskatoon. As an Associate Professor, she taught English for Academic Purposes for several years at the University of Nigeria, Nsukka.

She is the Founder and Executive Director of Giving Back Community Language Centre Inc., Saskatoon, Saskatchewan. She has supervised ESL programs and worked with the provincial government as a Career and Employment Consultant. She is a Scott Truitt Memorial Book-Prize Award winner, a Fulbright Scholar, international speaker at Urbana Champaign and International Christian Student conferences and presenter at numerous academic conferences such as ACCUTE and TESL. She has published articles in peer-reviewed journals, contributed to books, and published poems as well as a playlet that was performed in 2012.

She published a novel, *Just for Mercy* (Mercy Series Book 1), in 2016. She continues to write and to publish in different literary genres. She is an entrepreneur, running her own business as a financial guide. She and her husband own Pharmasave, Riversdale Pharmacy, Saskatoon. She is a successful wellness coach in the Ideal Protein Protocol. Along with her husband, they pastor a church in Saskatoon and are blessed with four amazing children.

Hannah Ngozi Eby Chukwu

Ph.D

THE ABILITY TO NAME ONESELF OR ONE'S GROUP IN THE CONTEXT OF ONE'S CULTURE AND EXPERIENCE IS ESSENTIAL FOR PSYCHOLOGICAL, SPIRITUAL, AND PHYSICAL EMPOWERMENT.

—Hannah Chukwu[13]

Chapter 9

BORN BUT MADE:

Defining Moments in my Leadership Journey

by Hannah Ngozi Eby Chukwu

Our innate predispositions along with our learning, growth, and development are responsible for our leadership abilities.[14] I believe that everyone is born with the potential to become a leader but only those with great self-control—who are able to establish a set of principles and faithfully follow them with self-discipline—can become true leaders. A leader is someone with a vision, that sets good examples for others to follow and considers others' welfare as much as their own. This is my story of how I learnt to master my emotions, grow as a person, find purpose in life and help others start their own leadership journey. My journey portrays my innate disposition. I was appointed a leader at a young age; various defining moments confirm the lessons I've learned, the growth I've undergone, and the influence I've had on others to achieve some goals and to effect a change.

Defining Moment: Early Leadership Years

One day in junior high school, I woke up like any fourteen-year-old girl, dressed in my school uniform, and attended a special afternoon assembly where I was given a new reality and identity—a leader. My name was announced as the new school Timekeeper (Bellringer). Other names were announced and appointed as prefects, but my name rang louder in my ears because I was thrust into a new light and given the responsibility of keeping the school system functioning. It showed me others' (fellow students and teachers) impression of me and how I would view myself in the future. That was a junior prefect position; the teachers and students had considered me worthy. It was an important occasion when new prefects were appointed. Something I never thought about or planned for had begun. I had been elected as a representative, to provide an example and to be seen as a responsible person, one to be emulated by other students.

Leadership was bestowed on students who had distinguished themselves academically and morally. I could not have planned for that. Nevertheless, I became a prefect. According to *Wiki How*, "Becoming prefect gives you the chance to help others in ways that you couldn't before and if you are a good prefect, people look up to you and want to be like you. You can inspire others into doing amazing things. It's also a good early taste of leadership and the responsibilities accompanying that."[15] My leadership journey began with the revelation that I am a leader, a role model in the school. As a young teen, I did not understand the challenges of leadership or even thought of it as a challenge. I later realized this when I began to have defining moments, revealing what I make of myself as a leader and the impact I could have on others. It's a journey with exulting moments, painful tears, numerous lonely times, but also triumph through growth and change. Reflecting on these excites and humbles me. It was a journey that revealed who I am, my motivation, and how I treat others.

According to John Maxwell, "A defining moment is a challenge or crisis that demonstrates the leadership capacity that lies inside a person."[16] From high school to today, defining moments have contributed to my strength and confidence. I was born a leader, but these moments demonstrate growth and development, based on my innate character. Every leadership experience without a crisis point is not true leadership. Leading other people takes courage, vision, patience, integrity, firmness in love, noble intentions, actions, and selflessness.

I had several crises in my leadership journey, but the greatest experience that revealed who I am and my innate qualities came two years later during my leadership as the Senior Prefect (SP) in my senior high school years. The experience shook me to the core and I was nearly destroyed. The truth remains that what does not kill you will make you stronger. At the peak of my leadership glory, my defining moment came.

As the leader of leaders, various opinions and questions were raised as to who I truly was and the value I brought. Some of my peers questioned my ability.

My friend came to summon me to an agitators' secret meeting. I trusted her so I walked in, the Senior Prefect of a school of over thousand students (day-students and boarders), the leader of forty prefects (thirty-eight of them were my peers and two my juniors). I was looked upon as the leader of leaders and the highest authority among the student body, recognized by the teachers, management staff, and principal. I was the Head Girl of the entire school and a spokesperson who represented the students and liaised with management and outside authority for any matter in the best interest of the students. I walked in not sure what the meeting was about; my confidence and courage sustained me. I used to refer to myself as an incurable optimist, born with the confidence that there's no situation without a solution, especially when God is involved.

"Sit over there," the spokesperson said, pointing to a chair by the side of a table on the platform. I sensed something was wrong because no prefect can tell a senior prefect what to do. As soon as I was seated, the spokesperson continued: "We have decided that you're no longer qualified to lead. You have aggrieved us, disrespected us, denied us our rights. We've reclaimed our rights; from now, we dethrone you and enthrone the Deputy Senior Prefect (DSP) as the Senior Prefect (SP)."

These words, even though very serious and grievous, might not have amounted to much because these prefects were appointed by the school authority (principal, vice principals, teachers, and student body) as I was. Therefore, a meeting chaired by the DSP was not enough to depose me of my position; however, it was a huge threat and a grave decision not to be ignored or taken lightly. The atmosphere was oppressively solemn and tense.

The unexpected had happened. I seemed unruffled on the outside, but my heart sank, and failure stared me in the face. I felt alone and abandoned, rejected, and exposed to shame and ridicule. I took a deep breath. I summoned up courage and said: "I'll like to know why you are doing this and what made you think you have the right to make these decisions." I acted as though I hadn't heard their stated reasons. I was dazed and had half expected to hear their accusations. I was aware of their resentment of me; I was not convinced I was guilty of what I was being accused of. I continued: "This is conspiracy. You mean that all of you thirty-eight prefects gathered and took this decision? Conspiracy, I call this! I demand you tell me what I did. What did I do to warrant this decision?"

Surprisingly, none spoke; a palpable silence ensued.

My previously trusted friend whom I had regarded as my sister in another term, and the one sent to invite me to the meeting, stood up and began to address me thus: "You see, Hannah, everyone is unhappy. You may not understand. The fact is that you have not represented our interests well enough. You have robbed us of our authority; therefore, we cannot continue to have you as our leader."

At that moment, I felt like Caesar betrayed by Brutus. Caesar couldn't believe what he was seeing so he said 'Et tu, Brute?[17] Then fall, Caesar.' It was also like when Judas led the captains and the army to betray Jesus with a kiss. My friend was neither Brutus, nor Judas but I felt betrayed, sold out, thrown under the bus; I wouldn't have come to the meeting if I hadn't trusted her. The prefects knew that and used her. As a Senior Prefect, you carry yourself with dignity and follow protocols as the situation demands. As the SP, I attend meetings with prior notice and knowledge.

I refused to fall like Caesar. When I'm badly shaken, like as I was that night, when wounded, and torn almost to pieces, a huge strength and confidence comes upon me. I seem to have an unending capacity to endure. I have often felt as though a special grace has been granted me to overlook pain and disappointment. I forget tears, fear, disgrace, and insult; rather a curious strength comes on me to persevere and to see the end with a positive outcome.

I sat there, very upset but in quiet resolve to be strong. But what would one person do to a group of leaders who were angry and ready to do the worst? A significant number of them were older than me. I was alone and they were united in their plot and decision. Badly hurt and disappointed, I kept quiet and wondered where this would end. The school had invested leadership of the school in me. Here were my fellow leaders rejecting me without any consideration or emotion. My thoughts were racing.

How would I function in maintaining discipline and order in the school with this kind of open dissent and declared battle? This was anarchy and confusion. Should I accept their proposal and write to the principal to resign and ask to become the DSP? That was not an option because it would have forced me to accept what I deemed wrong and to live with that pain for the rest of my life. Thoughts and questions were racing through my mind. The worst hurt was my friend's action and it cut deeper than any other. I must find a way through this and out of this.

Silence!

Finally, to end the silence, I found my voice and asked:

"How have I not led you well and how have I taken away your rights? Is it because I didn't want you to punish the junior students at will? Is sitting them out in the cold to repeat nonsense about themselves what you call your rights of leadership and maintenance of order? What wrong did I do?"

My friend responded: "Your problem is that you have a commanding tone!" Another matter-of-fact response from a friend! At that point I lost my voice and determined that this was deeper than I thought. I became silent.

Absolute silence in the face of hostility and conspiracy seemed to have helped me to catch my racing thoughts, to take a deep breath and, there and then, to make the decision to forge ahead against all odds and against deep-rooted and planned opposition. We lose our voices only to find them later! One doesn't begin to count one's miles until one gets to the finish line! Did I find my voice? I think I did.

The process of finding my voice will require going back to my background, birth, and experience before the crisis. I was born the last of nine surviving children. Indeed, I regard myself as the 10th born because I lost a sister and a twin brother in their infancy. I never knew them. I have a companion, actually a multitude behind me, whether visible or invisible.

I grew up without any sense of lack even though I didn't have everything I needed. I felt surrounded and shielded physically and spiritually and never lacked confidence.

As a child, I regarded my older aunty, my grandmother. She gave me a nickname that I didn't think much about then. She called me: "Obere ga abu nnukwu"[18]—the little one that shall become great. Recently, I have begun to think that that name is prophetic.

My parents were my exemplars regarding independence, thinking outside the box, and operating by vision because they were non-conformists and agents of change. What they accomplished, the positive influence they had with their level of education kept me humble and inspired me to be my best. My father served as a clergy and my mother was a kindergarten teacher. They had high school education as well as several in-house trainings for missionary work.

On becoming the SP, everything progressed well. I remember making my inaugural speech where I promised to do my best to make the school the best school, one to be envied by other schools. I was later informed that the speech was well-articulated. I didn't write any speech. I spoke when prompted to do so. I had peace and I flourished. Everyone cooperated. During one of the general assemblies, the Deputy Minister of Education and other dignitaries for the state visited the school to introduce a new program to help deal with the social causes of delinquency and dropouts. After his moving speech, I was called upon, without any warning, to give an impromptu thank-you speech. I still marvel at my confidence and composure. One thing I know about myself is that I'm not a self-conscious person. I can wear most leadership hats unassumingly by just being myself and speaking from my heart. After delivering the vote of thanks, the students and teachers went wild with their enthusiastic applause, more than they did for the Deputy Minister.

The principal called me into her office to praise me for the speech. The only thing I remember from the speech was that I praised the Deputy Minister for his selflessness. He had recently returned from the United States of America and was appointed to the position. I truly admired his hard work and knowledge-sharing; my appreciation was heart-felt. That was how I gained reputation by speaking well of others and appreciating them without any pretensions. This attitude has often gained me popularity in many circles.

As I continued in my leadership role as the SP into the next term, I observed some negative tendencies in the way junior students were being treated by the prefects in collaboration with some senior students. On some nights, an impromptu assembly would be called on the pretext that the students needed to be drilled to ensure they complied with the impeccable standards of discipline upheld by the prefects. I witnessed some of these meetings, but I observed that such a meeting was nothing more than oppression and was bound to depress rather than inspire the students. I observed that the prefects sometimes held such meetings with the DSP. One meeting that motivated me to take steps to ban it was when junior students were called after lights out and made to sit in the cold repeating negative words about themselves and to make promises to behave well. They make them sing songs like:

I'm a toad.
I'm a fresher.
I'm a rotten material.
I must obey all school rules
and regulations,
given by all prefects.

I advised my peers that this treatment must stop. They insisted it didn't. I had to act by releasing the students and telling them to go back to their hostels and to their beds. The ringleader for such meetings was my deputy and she felt offended. Soon after, I noticed that some prefects stopped minding me. When I called meetings, they didn't show up. Then some of the teachers sided with the prefects and turned against me. School harmony and order began to disintegrate.

On the outside, I kept strong and tried to do my best to avoid a complete breakdown of law and order. I upheld the standards by reminding the prefects that their duty of maintaining order was not dependant on their opinion of me. I felt so lonely and often cried on my bed, other times, silently as I walked through the school. No one wants to identify with a rejected leader. I walked to the dining hall alone. All I needed to do was to report them to the principal, but I knew what the consequence would be, so I didn't choose that fast and easy option. That was the situation until that night of the great conspiracy meeting, when the prefects, led by my deputy, announced that they were deposing me. The growing tension peaked that night.

When the conspiracy became clear and the battle line was drawn, I finally left the meeting and returned to my room. I prayed in tears and brokenness. I was a young Christian and often prayed and loved reading my Bible. I tried to organize a meeting after that. Some of them came but showed rudeness and negativity. I finally told them that since they had chosen to destroy law and order that I would be watching them and would continue to do my best. I told them to mark my words: "You're not right in what you wanted so be sure of this that your sins will surely find you out."[19]

That was it; a few weeks later, the senior hostel mistress, who was my deputy's staunch supporter, fell out with my deputy. From there, she took the case to the principal and told her how the prefects had done everything possible to break down law and order. She gave a full account of their negativism, insubordination, and uncooperative attitude they had unleashed on me and their other hidden destructive actions. The principal set up a disciplinary committee to investigate. Interestingly, no one called me as a witness because the senior hostel mistress knew everything and had said everything in my favour even though she was their staunch supporter in their rebellion. A significant number of the prefects were found guilty and were disciplined.

Leadership is a principle-based lifestyle. I learned from experience that the best leadership is to live and to lead by principle and not by convenience. I learned that the path to success and significance is strewn with tears and pain and a time must come when a leader has to stand alone without fear. I learned what it means to go against the grain and to risk everything for what is right. I was pushed to the wall and would have resorted to concession because of fear of rejection but because I was brought up to love justice and fairness, I was unable to agree with them.

I bore the suffering and loneliness with courage derived from my faith and comfort in God. I never let my parents know what was going on in the school. I thank God I survived, and God fought for me. I received a meritorious award as the best Senior Perfect and a virtuous woman book award when I graduated. To risk everything to stand for what is right is my leadership approach. My actions were revolutionary even though at that time I did not see myself as a revolutionist. To change a long-standing tradition, culture, or social order takes a leader with a vision. Bullying and other forms of abuse still happen, and it takes revolutionary leadership to fight and destroy the old order and set up a new one. That was what I did. Even though I suffered greatly, it was worth the fight and God helped me.

For young people today, one of the greatest fears is rejection by peers. Because of my principled leadership embedded in courage, integrity, fairness, and passion, peer pressure and rejection hurt me but my commitment to inspire, encourage, and to help others by making things better for them and to spare them so they don't suffer unnecessarily lessens the pain of rejection. The world would be a better place if every leader, at the risk of being hurt, strives for a change for the good of others.

My Ongoing Leadership Growth

Negotiation is one quality of leadership I'm learning in my career and my home. In my high school experience, I was aware of justice and equity, integrity, care for others, selflessness, truth, and courage. Negotiation is something I didn't intentionally practise or understand until my next level of leadership journey where I had to lead other leaders in a professional setting. The same principle of leading through fairness, courage, and example applies to my recent leadership experiences. One of the toughest things I did was to blaze the trail for my family by leaving the comforts of Nigeria in 2002 to undertake a journey of faith and coming to Canada. It was not the first time I had traveled outside Nigeria and battled with sadness for leaving home. The first was in 1996 when I won the Fulbright Junior Scholarship Award to pursue a research program for my doctorate degree first at the University of California, Davies and then at the University of Wisconsin, Madison. Coming to Canada was different because it was longer than my one-year faculty experience in the United States of America. I came to Canada as a graduate student, shortly before I bagged my doctorate degree in Nigeria. I was misunderstood and highly criticized because people did not understand why a woman, a wife, a mother would leave home to make a way for the family. I remember crying every day for seven days because of the pain of being alone and going through the normal challenges most black immigrants face with regards to subtle and obvious racism. I would have been suffering from depression, but I'm amazed and grateful for the grace of God that turned my sacrifice into a huge opportunity for my family. God also planted some friends in my life to support me. Chief among them include Doreen Stumborg and her family. They have become a life-long family friends. Some professors at the University of Saskatchewan, Saskatoon such as Profs. Janice Fiamengo, Susan Gingell, Patience Elabor-Idemudia and Ike Oguocha also became good friends.

I finished my studies; worked in the field of English as a Second Language (ESL) and coordinated work placements as a liaison officer for immigrants and refugees in professional fields. Later, I went back to Nigeria to teach for one year to repay the kindness for the support I received. Years later, my family and I became permanent residents of Canada. After working as a consultant with the government, managing training program contracts, I became a coordinator of ESL training programs, authoring reports to the government, and being responsible for supervising several staff delivering the programs. In any position I hold, I am proactive in bringing improvements in terms of fulfilling the mission and simplifying the process for the people I'm leading. For instance, when I managed a training program for the government, I made sure the program was enhanced by seeking solutions and pushing for policies to help make the system more effective in delivering the programs.

As a coordinator of ESL training programs, I knew I had to work hard and be ahead of the group so that I could improve myself and continue to be relevant as a leader. I had a very blissful career. In fact, one of my colleagues nicknamed me "Sunshine." Everyone was singing my praises, but I was careful because I had a feeling that humans change a lot and may not always be depended upon. It may take just one negative person to poison the minds of others and the euphoria of a wonderful cordial relationship will fall apart. I was thankful and humbled by how well the programs were going and flourishing better than they had before I came. I was conscious about not taking all the credit for myself but careful to give praise to whom it was due. I produced materials that the organisation is still distributing to other organisations to help them, and I created systems to make the process duplicatable for sustainable success. However, one of my friends used to tease me that I have a biting ant in my socks, as I don't like being in any position for too long. I'm always on the move to challenge myself. I usually will give myself one year to get established, change things for the better and to achieve significance. Then I work the system until it becomes strong and better. Next, I begin to look for another challenge. I stayed in the position for less than two years for several reasons.

As the coordinator of the ESL training programs, the program grew and received funding. My boss, staff and clients were all impressed. I cleared the backlog of government reports. I prepared reference materials to help make the system more efficient and to minimize confusion, delays, and errors. I designed many reporting templates to make the numerous reports manageable for the staff. I was working very hard and putting in extra time. I trained volunteers to assist me since I was denied an assistant in the position even though my contract indicated that I should have one. Later, when I moved on from the position, my successor had two assistants hired to help her. It was all good because one of the volunteers I mentored eventually advanced to occupy a similar position in a sister organisation and has become one of the board of directors for the Canadian Language Benchmark.

It is ironic that when you do well your boss is not necessarily pleased with you. Sometimes, the success of others produces jealousy and negative reactions. My boss wanted to know why I had such tremendous success and why she didn't get the same staff cooperation as I did. I knew why; I pray about everything and work hard. One ingrained leadership principle I have is to treat others as I would like to be treated. Part of my purpose as a leader is to inspire and to encourage others. Also, I have to lead by example and show my staff that they matter and are important to me. I applied these values both in responding to my staff and in staff evaluations. In one staff evaluation, even when my boss instructed me to be harsh, I focused on fairness and truth, without bias. We often offend others so why would I use bias to deny someone his or her promotion? That is human but that is not leadership. A leader is expected to manage not only human frailty but her own negative tendencies and to inspire others to take the higher road.

I also learned that people's betrayal of others is common. Therefore, in the staff evaluation, my boss wanted me to fail the staff member. I went ahead to do the job as it should be done. I pointed out to the employee all the good things she did and praised her for them. I used specific examples for some areas needing improvement. To inspire her, I connected her skills and abilities to what the future might hold for her in the profession. I researched and outlined helpful resources. At the end, I offered her assistance and invited her to talk with me and to ask for help. I recommended her for promotion with strong points. Truth be known, this staff had rubbed me the wrong way several times. She had incited arguments during meetings and rudely interrupted me. I had handled those well and still had the meetings in control. My practice is to invite the person later privately for a discussion to ascertain why the person was doing what she or he did at the meeting. However, before I could invite her to meet with me in my office, she took the initiative and informed the other staff that she was wrong in her attitude at the meeting. She encouraged them to dismiss what she said. She sent an email, copied to me, advising them to cooperate with me in the direction I was leading. I was encouraged and saw her as someone capable of doing well when her leader responds to her negativism with the right attitude. Of course, that is not often easy for a leader to do. This same staff had once informed me in the presence of everyone that because I had delayed in bringing a rented van to take everyone to a conference, out of town, that she would never forgive me. Although I was sure she has also aggravated my boss, I was not aware how matters were handled between them. I don't listen to gossip. If I hear gossip, I'll simply tell the informant, "I'll mention your name when I ask the person about what you said." Most times, gossipers don't like that.

My boss was one of those sophisticated smart ladies who likes to be in control and to be recognized as the boss who must be obeyed. After I submitted my report and recommended the staff for promotion, my boss was disappointed with my report because it was not what she wanted. Therefore, during the evaluation meeting among my boss, the staff and me, my boss suddenly turned against me, criticizing the suggestions I made for improvement and informed the staff that my suggestions made no sense and that she would never have done those herself. I kept quiet and inwardly thanked God that I didn't take her advice to be negative. I knew the report was impeccable so I didn't have any reason to defend anything or to feel ashamed, so the staff was promoted. As soon as the meeting was over, I left, disgusted at the negative attitude, but at the same time bursting with laughter and grateful to God because I would have become a fool if I had listened to my boss and given a manipulated report about my staff member. I was shocked at how ridiculous and meaningless life could be when we try to please other people. I was happy because I promised myself that next time, if my boss asked me to do her dirty job that I would remind her about this situation. She sensed her ridiculous actions, so she came to my office to apologise, telling me she didn't know what came upon her at the meeting. I respected her for coming to apologize; however, I wanted to tell her that nothing came upon her but that she was just being human, changeable, and self-important, but I held my tongue. I accepted her apology but was sure I was dealing with someone I could not trust. Trust is a huge thing in leadership.

I frequently read and meditate on the Bible. I've always been fascinated by Daniel, one of the three top officials in the Babylonian kingdom. It was said that his work was so perfect that no fault was found with it. I adopted that attitude and often strive to do my work with no errors at all. I believe in working hard and praying hard. Therefore, I maintained my good relationship with the staff and kept doing my best to treat them the same way I would like to be treated. Treating everyone fairly is my principle for life—doing to others what I would like to be done to me. One puzzling behaviour that I find among some Black people in position of leadership is to treat other Blacks with less respect and to treat people of other races with greater respect. That behaviour is both incomprehensible and repulsive to me. I kept an open-door policy. I talked things over and addressed issues in the best possible way I could and with respect. I apologized when wrong. However, as a leader, I focus on having a zero tolerance of my own mistakes because I recognize that although one may apologize, it doesn't correct the error; moreover, some people can be unforgiving and will remember mistakes for a long time. I go the extra mile to do things right the first time, but, at the same time am willing to apologize when necessary. My boss wasn't pleased because I maintained a great relationship with the staff members while her relationship with them was going nowhere.

Leading the staff was not easy. The time I hurriedly put out a document for discussion without checking it over, most of the staff began to correct my English and pointed out one error after another and concluded that my document was poorly written and difficult to discuss. When I looked at the errors, I thought they were minor but as a leader I hold myself accountable. One of the errors was using a singular noun when I should have used a plural. I was rattled but I looked all of them straight on and said, "They that live in glass houses should not throw stones." They understood me and softened their negative stance. I saw all their errors and corrected them, so my words were warning to them not to overact. Sometimes, I disagreed with them, but we agreed to disagree, and things were good, and the programs were flourishing. I was receiving affirmations and support. My boss was restless. She called a secret meeting of the staff to ask them to report some negative things I did. Surprisingly, they praised me rather than said anything negative. She kept questioning them, but their feedback was positive, and they affirmed that they were satisfied with my leadership.

I did not know about this until an African sister and staff member informed me about the secret meeting and what had transpired. African sisters know what it means to be a woman of colour. Friendship among women is priceless. The staff were mostly white and female but my friendship, mutual respect, and communication with them was healthy irrespective of colour. Those staff members made me proud during the secret meeting planned to discredit and malign me and destroy my good works. However, none of them told me about the secret meeting except my fellow African sister who was new. She told me because she was impressed. My secret for success is simply to demonstrate my faith in Jesus through what I do.

I'm a straightforward person who says things the way they are. I think that may be one of the reasons my boss was afraid of me and didn't like me very much. I like to be open, friendly, and sincere but hate to compromise or hide my intentions. However, I'm learning that diplomacy and lobbying can be helpful when dealing with people who may resent your success. That is the next level of leadership I want to master and apply in my current engagement as a director and business owner.

A Work In Progress With Success Along The Way

I have continued in the same spirit of fearless leadership and living life with passion, striving to encourage and make things better for others. In 2012, my husband wanted to open his own pharmacy but was stymied by the bank. In 2014, I joined Primerica and learned financial principles. We applied Primerica's well-proven concepts, abolished our debts and built equity. I am currently building a solid financial business that will serve numerous financially educated independent families and businesses. On December 15, 2017, Pharmasave, Riversdale Pharmacy was born; after five years, we have built a business that is debt-free and constantly growing because we put our faith to work and God gave the increase. My husband and I were the only full-time staff of Pharmasave, Riversdale Pharmacy along with our children who worked part-time while they were in school. To date, we have hired over thirty staff. I had no previous Canadian retail experience, but today, I am the go-to-person in areas dealing with human resources, cash-handling, purchasing, workflow, organisation, growth, as well as a wellness coach in our Ideal Protein Program. We pride ourselves in giving first opportunities to newcomers who lack Canadian work experience. We operate an open-door policy and treat our staff as a family with respect and professionalism. Our goal is to be the best community pharmacy in the area by creating a generative win-win situation among our staff, clients, and community to achieve economic growth and independence.

I still have many goals to pursue beyond consolidating our family business in retail pharmacy. Chief among them is to be an established author. In 2016, I published my first novel, *Just for Mercy*, a huge breakthrough. When I was nineteen years old, I had my first completed manuscript in drama, but it got destroyed in a house fire. It took a couple of decades to have another completed manuscript now in fiction. My first novel is the kind of book I like to read—real stories of faith, entrepreneurship, and significance amid challenges and trials. It was a dream come true to the glory of God. As I sat down for an interview with Darlene Polachic, a journalist from the local Saskatoon daily newspaper, The *Star Phoenix*, published on March 5, 2016, I recall my motivation for writing as revealed in the title of the published interview: "Chukwu Goes against the Norm in her Inspirational Book." I also gave an interview on Saskatoon's community radio CFCR 90.5FM.

In preparation to launch the book, I had a press release, with the theme, "The Spiritual Collides with the Physical to Birth a Resonate Hope: The Efficacy of a Nurturing Community." March 12, 2016 was the book launch that attracted over three hundred people from around Saskatchewan as well as the then Mayor of Saskatoon. I also had the privilege to sign a copy of my book for the current Mayor of Saskatoon at a community event. I worked hard for these successes, with many helpers. In 2017, I incorporated my not-for-profit organisation called Giving Back Community Language Centre in the bid to help create more spaces for immigrants and refugees to become integrated in the community and workforce.

My leadership experiences have taught me that living by principle makes life simpler and helps to develop purposefulness, howbeit, God's purpose to bless me and to make me a blessing to others. Principle is the way to go. I've learned that leadership is a challenge and a call to become better not just for others but for myself. I was born to lead but my success and impact as a leader is being accomplished through a combination of who I am, my growth in the face of challenges, my faith as tested and proven in defining moments, and the help I receive from God to have an impact and influence others towards achieving a goal. The best is yet to come as I continue to be a leader by example in faith, gratitude lifestyle, courage, and integrity and much more encouragement to others so that they too can become the leaders of their dreams.

Meet The Author

Rose Kumbu is the CEO, owner and Executive Chef of Rosaly's Food Services Inc. Her packaged food products are sold all across Saskatoon and Alberta. She has received an Award from the Congolese Canadian Women's Association of Toronto, Ontario as one of the youngest Black African entrepreneurs and one of 100 women to watch for award winner 2016.

She is the vice president of la CECS (conseil economique et du développement de la saskatchewan) where she has been active for the past 7 years, she is presently an ambassador for U.N.A.C (United Nations Canada Saskatoon branch). She is the founder of She Got It, a women entrepreneur for leadership and mentorship advocacy community.

She is also the founder and a board of director of My Humanitas, a platform for foster children in Saskatoon. She is a member and a leader in her church JIL (Jesus is Lord Edmonton west main), where she serves as a praise and worship leader and also in charge of the kitchen ministry and helps with the women ministry.

Rose Kumbu

IN THEIR HEARTS HUMANS PLAN THEIR COURSE, BUT THE LORD ESTABLISHES THEIR STEPS.

– Proverbs 16:9

Chapter 10

CALLED TO LEAD

by Rose Kumbu

I come from the French-speaking Democratic Republic of the Congo, once known as Zaire. I was born in 1974 in Matadi, which is well-known for being the country's main port and one of central Africa's largest ports. It is situated at the foot of the crystal mountains and has a mile-long granite waterfront. My parents gave me the names Rose Mputu Masambombo, Masambombo Ngandu Yoki Simon, a Congo notary, and Biakasasa Valentine Muambayi, a school principal and a professional tailor.

I was a vibrant, active little girl with thirty-five siblings, born to four different mothers. In Africa, some wealthy men frequently had multiple wives. My birth mother had nine children, and I am the third. Growing up, being surrounded by so many people was fun. I never experienced loneliness; my heart was filled with family members. It was bizarre at times, but I'll save that for another tale. This time, I'd like to talk about my struggles and how I overcame them to become an immigrant African descendant leader and businesswoman.

I began working as my father's secretary shortly after receiving my high school diploma at seventeen. He was the sole notary of Congo then, a position held by no one else in the nation. My father was a respected and well-known politician and a successful businessman. He motivated me to pursue my degree and grow into the capable businesswoman I am today.

My Entrepreneurial Roots

My passion for entrepreneurship started in grade eleven, when I began to receive my weekly allowances. I would cook boiled eggs to sell to my school friends and would go to the store to buy makeup, that would multiply my allowance, buy some gold jewelry, and sell it to my loved ones. I began my first business when I was eighteen. My father opened a little convenience store for me next to our house.

My father then started telling me about his coffee business and diamond trading. Since I was the one who recorded the AGM on camera, he also agreed to allow me to attend his political gatherings. I was merely getting to know him better and questioning his wisdom. Unfortunately, when his political career was at its peak, he became severely ill. At about the same time, I had to relocate to continue my microeconomics studies in Tunisia. Later, we learned that he had been battling prostate cancer for a few years. After I left the Congo in September 1996 and my father passed away in January 1997, everything changed. I could not complete my school in Tunisia because I lacked the money to cover my tuition. Around the same time, the rebels arrived in Congo. My eldest brother was already in Canada, where they were allowing immigrants. As it was difficult for me to return home, given that I am the daughter of a politician, I arrived in Montreal, spent a month with my cousins, and then joined my brother in Calgary, Alberta.

This portion of my journey did not appeal to me. I was a young, independent lady who desired to build a successful career in business. Instead, I had to rely on social welfare services in Canada, which was draining and frustrating. Without any money, I had to start over by learning the English language and the system. Power, influence, money, and even my friends and family had vanished, leaving me with nothing to lean on. However, I still had some hope because I grew up learning about the Lord Jesus Christ. My elder brother and I worked in manufacturing to support our mother and our other siblings, who were still living in the Congo under rebel rule.

Developing a Work Ethic and Acquiring Knowledge

I continued to have dreams—many dreams. But I knew that if I did nothing, I would have to spend the rest of my life working in the manufacturing industry. So I moved away from my brother so I could study in Ottawa. In addition, one of my sisters, who was living in the USA, had come to live with us in Canada. We both strongly committed to attending school, so she relocated to Ottawa with me.

To support myself, my mother and my siblings back home, I had to do various jobs while going to school and generate side businesses. From Tuesday through Saturday after school, I worked part-time as the manager and head chef at a restaurant. I also worked part-time as a childcare provider on Mondays and Sundays and for Molly Maid cleaning homes. It was a lot to have three jobs in addition to attending school, helping our mother move my other siblings out of the Congo, and contributing to their school expenses in US dollars. So I resolved to create a home daycare with the cash I had set up from my part-time jobs after completing my studies in early childhood education level two and year one of office administration. I also opened a home daycare where I lived with my sister and another brother who had joined us from the Congo that year.

Aside from the daycare business, I practiced as a hair braider and a bartender for six years while pursuing my business administration degree. Due to my repeated participation in demanding activities without any breaks, I eventually got physically and mentally exhausted. My health suffered as a result, which caused me to lose weight unhealthily and feel miserable. I wished I had a mentor and confidant at that time, but I didn't. I began smoking to feel better and relieve the stress, but as a Christian, I felt terrible as I wanted to be a good example for my siblings. I started doing community service to develop my work ethic, contacts, relationships, and friendships.

I began packaging my ginger juice and hot sauce in 1998 to give to my friends. I received my permanent residence three years after my arrival in Canada in 2000. I met my spouse, Ali, through ministering and our home gatherings. Ali was one of my cousin's friends who would join him to practice religion in our basement. While we both wanted to challenge ourselves to stop our unhealthy behaviours – my smoking addiction and his drinking - we were unable to do so on our own. So we decided to attend a retreat planned by our church since he also wanted to learn how to build a relationship with Christ. I stopped smoking during this long weekend of prayer, and Ali was baptized. Our twenty-four years of healthy lifestyle with the Lord at the heart of our every choice began with this healing miracle.

In 2000, we got engaged, and I kept working on my education. Ali was a Bell Sympatico employee. I still had a few months to complete both my early childhood education level three and my business administration diploma. I was hoping you wouldn't ask me why, but I did receive two diplomas in the same year. I knew I could succeed. That's what immigrants do: we put in additional effort to support our family back home as soon as possible. We had our traditional wedding in Congo at the end of 2000. Since we could not return to our country, we asked our siblings to represent us to both families. In the first week of September 2001, we got married in Canada.

In the same year, I completed my Early Childhood Education degree. Then, I began a new chapter of my life with a partner and an incredible friend. I didn't have to face this life alone. We felt fortunate. After I graduated, we moved into our first one-bedroom apartment. I then applied for my first job as a professional in Canada. Although I was the only woman and Black person employed as a clerk for a car dealer, it was scary. I believed I needed to prove myself more and have a particular mindset to avoid being intimidated.

We spent less than a week on our honeymoon, then September 11, 2001, took place—New York City's Twin Towers were destroyed. Later that month, we received the happy news that I was pregnant. But as things were breaking down in society, so were things in our personal lives. In October, we both lost our jobs, and in November, we also lost our baby. It was a time for stillness and reflection. Our marriage was severely tested. We were both in low spiritual places and unsure if we would be able to continue together. Thank God for my incredible mother, a prayer warrior, who has been a terrific mentor to me. My mother was a lovely woman of God who supported us at every turn. She would phone from Congo and join us in prayer. She had to buy phone cards to call as neither Skype nor WhatsApp helped our connection.

My husband had previously lived in Toronto, so we moved there hoping to find excellent employment. Instead, with access to a wider market in Toronto, I decided to rediscover my early ambitions of being a prosperous businesswoman.

Starting a business in Canada took a lot of work. I arrived in Canada as a refugee, and it took me nearly five years to become a citizen. Because of my position at the time, I could not do much about my dreams. I was focused on returning to school to become an office manager. When I was prepared to start a business, I started educating myself by reading books on business startups and increasing my understanding of nutrition. One of my mother's favorite books was recipe books. She comes from three generations of excellent cooks, as far as I can recall. I kept noticing her reading those books, so I started collecting them. Google and YouTube had just been created and made my life easier. They were the place where I could get all my questions answered. They served as my educators as well. But these platforms eventually turned into time wasters for me as I continuously spent hours, days, and nights researching and evaluating. Finally, I decided to be more purposeful and looked for inspirational speakers like Oprah, T.D. Jakes, and Joel Osteen; their videos were essentially "unknown" mentorship. Thanks to technology, I could see that there was still light at the end of the tunnel.

Building a family, Entrepreneurship and Financial Success

Although knowledge is essential for success, only money can achieve the latter. So I started participating in outdoor events to promote myself since we needed to raise money. That was when I decided to open a catering company. I loved making others happy, so I immediately fell in love with what I was doing.

Around that time and after life-threatening difficulties for both the unborn child and me during the unexpected pregnancy, we were blessed with a healthy baby girl. We named her Siloe, which means sent by God to accomplish. Today, she is a phenomenal athlete working toward her Olympic goal. In 2023, she will enroll in the University of Alberta to pursue a bachelor's degree in Kinesiology and Education. I have faith that she'll accomplish her goals.

I finished my business administration degree after Siloe was born, registered Rosaly's Food Services, our first business, and started our home daycare in Mississauga as a home-based organisation. Five children, including our daughter, were under our care. I used the Ontario School Board's curriculum to teach them English and French and scheduled music days, which the parents embraced.

Again, everything was perfect up until my father-in-law passed away. He was a tremendous patriot who treated me like his own daughter and loved, supported, and encouraged me. It was a difficult time for my husband, who could not see his father as he lacked the proper paperwork to travel abroad even though he had been in Canada for more than ten years. And it was a particularly challenging time for all of us as I was expecting our second child by then. Given my first pregnancy experience, I'm thankful that God kept me safe during this second pregnancy so I could give birth to Amzi, another healthy baby girl. Her name translates to "God strengthens." Today, she enjoys the arts and reading books and wishes to work as a film producer and director.

When our family was growing and I was establishing my businesses, my mother was recovering from a brain injury. The added stress was soon replaced by the sorrow of losing her three years later. However, she had been a constant presence in our lives, even from afar. She would call often and send us handmade clothing, meals, and encouraging notes anytime a friend or relative traveled from the Congo to Canada.

We grew closer as an empowered family because of these hardships and the loss of loved ones. We had friends who supported us as we expanded our small family. For five more years, I kept up my in-home childcare, providing a safe environment for our bilingual French and English children to grow up. Back in 2008, when I first started packaging my first two items (ginger and hot sauce) to sell to parents, friends, and others, I had yet to learn how to build a brand. So I had to start looking into it. However, at about the same time, my husband received a job offer in Saskatoon, so we decided to relocate there.

Another New Beginning and More Sacrifice

We had to start from nothing again. I started hosting outdoor events, advertising my catering company, and slowly, one by one, buying my equipment. Every time I went to the bank to apply for a loan, they told me I didn't have enough credit history. I thought that not having credit was a good thing. I never had one, but according to the bank, I needed to have some debt for them to give me some money so I could be in more debt!

I put in a bit more effort to create a business without taking on debt and needing the bank's funding. Over four years, I competed in different outdoor events. My children assisted since they were old enough, but I still put in extra hours and lived on little sleep. My husband would accompany me to these activities when he got home. Finally, we decided to live in cooperative housing to save more money for our goals. Unfortunately, we lived in a poor neighborhood with a house filled with cockroaches. The sight of my crying children, unable to close their eyes for fear of the insects, tortured me. However, with all our funds being invested in our Saskatoon company, we had to sacrifice to get back on our feet.

Sometimes I would cry thinking about who I was and where I had come from. Thinking of the times when my father gave me everything until I lived in poverty and worked hard to become prosperous. I cried because I no longer had those luxuries and missed how they made me feel. I wanted to provide my kids with the same life I had when I was a child. But I knew that time was at stake. Every day I watched them grow, and then, just as things were getting better, we had to start over.

2016 came with more hardship. I learned that I had a brain tumor. I had to stop my entire plan. I had recently concluded my project with the Savvy program for a grant that would have helped our business go into mass production and commercially take the brand to the next level, but I didn't have a backup strategy. Unfortunately, I became ill and was unable to complete the assignment. Fortunately, the same year I was diagnosed, I also released my first product into the market—the Beignets mix—which had been developing for the previous three years. It was an amazing product.

Although we had insurance, it didn't cover my prescriptions, and we didn't have enough money in the bank at the time. My husband had to give up his job to care for me. Every day, the pleasure of the Lord was our strength, so we kept a smile on our faces for our daughters and were spiritually strong. Several wonderful friends actively prayed for us and kept a close eye on our children. I remained unemployed for four years. I couldn't walk by myself. I moved around in a wheelchair. And although I was meant to be paralyzed, yet again, I overcame following my surgery. While in a coma, I had an extraordinary meeting with my Savior. I firmly believe what the Bible says about faith being certainty about what we do not see (Hebrews 11:1). I briefly visited heaven. Heaven exists.

Eventually, two years following my surgery, I returned to work performing light duties. I was not allowed to carry anything or engage in any physical activity. I felt worthless. I wanted to move around and accomplish things, but it was challenging. During that time, I gained knowledge. Life is not a race, so there is no point in trying to win it. Take each day as it comes. Enjoy the process, and be grateful for each step you take. Even though you might not have recognized it as a learning experience at the time, as the days pass, you will realize that every circumstance is a teaching opportunity. Your actions may depend on what you learn from it. Thankfully, I already owned most of my kitchen equipment. I just had a few things I needed to buy to run the business. I wasn't concerned with how quickly or skillfully I performed this time. Along the way, I had a few mentors who also assisted in bringing together the people who are now my adoptive family. They helped me realize my dream of opening a restaurant.

Sadly, my eldest sister passed away a year after we opened the restaurant. COVID-19 came along when I returned to the Congo for her funeral. I spent over two months isolated in Congo due to the lockdown. When I returned, we had to close the restaurant because the building owner wanted to construct a parking lot. It was challenging because the same month after our return, my brother, who had traveled with me to bury our sister in Congo, passed away. Yet I kept on going. I needed not to take it personally for the sake of my family. Once again, I had to restart. The opportunity my family had with our children's education—one starting university and the other in high school—and my husband's job as an RCMP in training led us to relocate to Alberta.

Looking Back and Looking Forward

The hardest part of my journey has been getting the information I needed from others. Since no one will look at you if you can't show them the money, I was consistently ignored, denigrated, mistreated, and given little to no attention. You had to meet a specific threshold to be considered a part of some groups' environment. Even though that wasn't the case in every office I visited, I continued to wonder if the reason I received different treatment was due to my gender or skin tone. But I pressed on regardless. My goals were clear to me.

Launching my first product, Rosaly's African Beignets and pancake and waffle dry mix, was a significant accomplishment for me as an entrepreneur. The foremost food expert I met with at a government organisation to complete my branding requirement determined that I lacked the financial resources to create the brand required for use in retail stores. I wouldn't even be offered a chair to sit on when I went to the consultant's office. I would schedule my appointment weeks in advance, but on the day of the appointment, the office would be closed, so I would have to wait outside. Some of the agency's other departments didn't answer their phones or respond to emails. But I never lost sight of my goals. The situation saddened me, but I didn't feel inferior.

On the contrary, I prayed while I worked to get my product on the market. Therefore, I was genuinely happy to meet Sara Lui and her staff at the Food Center. I obtained all the information required to have my brand certified and my label released into the market thanks to Sara's friendship, support, and the knowledge of her team.

Even though I currently reside in Alberta, Saskatchewan will always be my home because it is where I raised my children and founded my business. In Saskatchewan, we introduced two products: the pancake, beignet, and waffle mix in 2017. Rosaly's was officially incorporated in 2019.

In 2023, we will introduce five additional goods to the market. To expand into mass production, we are working on a project to construct our own manufacturing facility. I've gone back to school and am pursuing a two-year degree in business management and trades. "Educating oneself is a continuance of increasing your area," as my father used to say.

Our company's goal is to become a family-owned African-descendant enterprise that serves Canadian and global markets. We strive to create a complete line of goods inspired by the culinary or ethnic richness of Africa. We have five staff, and in late summer 2022, we introduced our hibiscus and ginger beverages. Despite obstacles that delay our goals and cause us to lose hope, if we have faith in ourselves, we will still succeed.

This is my life story. While I am a flawed Black woman, we all share the same red blood. You see me as strong because life has turned me into a warrior. I've experienced challenging times, therefore I'm vulnerable. I possess intelligence and a wealth of spiritual wisdom. Without a good education, I can do anything. Despite being referred to as a minority, I am the majority. I may not be wealthy, but I am strong, blessed, and highly favored. Like my father used to say, "I am a rare flower that's hard to get because I am gorgeous and brilliantly formed." I am a child of the Most High, the Great One. I am Rose, an African descendant from an equatorial region of the world living in Canada. I am a Black woman, but most importantly, I am a child of God.

YOUR DREAMS MAY BE DELAYED BY LIFE CIRCUMSTANCES BUT YOUR DESTINY SHALL COME TO PASS, JUST BELIEVE

– Rose Kumbu

Meet The Author

Bukola is an entrepreneur, a former banker, certified relationship coach, Natural Wellness Expert, and a clinical Administrative Assistant.

She is the founder of Ibiss Love Haven, a relationship and marriage platform. She is also the founder of Ibiss Natural Wellness for all kinds of health and wellness products for skin, hair and general wellness.

She is currently pursuing another degree in Social Work and plans to focus her practice on family, marriage. and mental health. She has had a long battle with imposter syndrome as a result of bullying and she has taken it upon herself to be a voice against it and any form of injustice affecting people's mental health.

Bukola Udefiagbon

"

DO NOT ALLOW THAT LITTLE TINY VOICE, WHISPERING YOUR INADEQUACIES TO YOU, STOP YOU FROM BIRTHING GREATNESS

– Bukola Udefiagbon

Chapter 11

OVERCOMING THE IMPOSTER SYNDROME

by Bukola Udefiagbon

They say that life is not a bed of roses. I agree with that statement, especially for those facing internal barriers, such as the battle with imposter syndrome; this common phenomenon limits success in life and leadership. I wondered if people with skin-colour advantage, the right socioeconomic background, or who were raised in developed countries with 'privileges' faced similar problems. For me, life has been a battle for survival. I have had to fight, struggle, and work hard to battle the imposter syndrome to get things done. What an irony of life!

Am I Good Enough?

My name is Bukola Udefiagbon, Née Owoeye. I was born into a family of six, with four girls and two boys. I studied Banking and Finance at the Federal Polytechnic Bida and Lagos State Polytechnic, respectively, in Nigeria, to obtain my first degree. After completing my studies, I served for one year at the National Youth Service Corps (NYSC).

Right from childhood, I have been versatile, strong-willed, and a go-getter. I have the innate capabilities to do many things, such as modelling, acting, singing, dancing, and public speaking. My talents, skills, and attributes drew people to me and made me popular in the schools that I attended and the organisations where I worked. I love people and relate well with others. Most people assume that I am extroverted, very vocal, and outgoing. I consider myself a 'burden bearer'—I love to support people, especially when they are going through a difficult time, by offering a listening ear and encouraging and empowering them to overcome life challenges. My mantra is, "no mountain is too high for me to crumble or climb." Achieving leadership positions at work and in my community was easy because people believed I was capable and reliable. People consider me to be a natural leader. My mirror became my best friend. I would always say my affirmations while standing in front of my mirror.

As I grew in wisdom and stature, I got involved in different leadership roles. As a result, I was exposed to various and diverse obligations. As a result, I gained better clarity about the numerous things I could do. However, soon after, confusion, fear, misalignment of purpose, and, most significantly, listening to people who did not understand my purpose in life started to hinder me. I focused on the voices of people who did not understand my goals and ambitions, which led to the IMPOSTER SYNDROME. Imposter syndrome is the persistent inability to believe that one's success is well deserved. It's an inner voice that critiques one's efforts and abilities, making you feel unworthy. Who would have thought that an outspoken and passionate person with the ability to inspire and influence others would suffer from imposter syndrome? Whenever I had the opportunity to address or impact a gathering of people, I received comments such as: "Awesome job, well done!" applause and appreciation. I recall one particular instance when I presented some data we had collected as a team. The audience well received the presentation, and I received great feedback.

However, my inner critic ramped up instead of acknowledging the positive comments. I did not provide good examples or enough information or appeared well composed. I felt undeserving and persistently believed that my efforts or skills were not rightfully achieved. Even though I always gave my best, I would come back home and break down, question my abilities, talk myself down, and complain to the mirror about things I could have done better or that I missed. Even though I was applauded, I would question the lasting impression I gave the audience - "What if someone didn't like my appearance or my speech?" I was never fulfilled and happy. I would torment myself with all these negative thoughts. I would break down because I had this false judgement of myself, which I projected onto the audience. These are the classic symptoms of imposter syndrome.

The proverbial statement that always popped into my mind was "a jack of all trades is a master of none." This statement tortured me for years because it made me doubt my abilities and gifts that I had and caused me to feel like a fraud. As a result, my mirror became my best friend and a safe place to vent. I would stand in front of the mirror and speak words of affirmation to feel better. Finally, years later, I understood the proverbial torturous statement, "a jack of all trades is a master of none though often better than a master of one." - Anonymous.

Seeking Fulfilment

My imposter syndrome aside, I was doing well in every other aspect of my life. I married the most committed, loyal, and caring man ever. He is a person who would go miles to make me happy. I was financially stable and doing well in my career, yet I did not feel fulfilled because it was not my core purpose. I became hard on myself, allowing the thoughts and opinions of other people to weigh me down. I felt incompetent whenever I tried a new venture. I was consumed with the views of those who did not understand my purpose. It was ongoing and all-consuming. My filters selectively curated the messages that seemed to reinforce the belief that I was not good enough. It felt like a setup! I began to self-sabotage with my negative self-talk and inner critic.

I would ask myself: "How can you know how to do so many things? Are you a jack of all trades, master of none? What can unfinished products achieve? What can come out of you? Do you need to be more experienced? Yes, you proffer solutions that work, but that's guesswork. Your community doesn't need you now because they have better and more capable hands. Go and learn to be better before achieving a fulfilling career as a strong speaker, leader, or relationship coach to singles and married people." These and many more thoughts were my daily struggles, and of course, my mirror was nearby to listen to my negative self-talk. "But, hey, mirror, I'm still here." Laughs!

One day, I was standing in front of the mirror, as always, staring at my reflection, when I heard a voice speaking distinctly to me, saying, "It's just you here and your maker (God); I created you beautifully and wonderfully to fulfil a purpose, to impact both the old and young, to encourage and lead people to self-discovery and attainment of their purpose. I want you to be a blessing to marriages and relationships. Why, then, do you struggle and doubt your abilities? I have deposited those abilities in you freely because I know you are capable. Still, here you are complaining to yourself, aren't you in the mirror? You are the solution, and you are also the problem; choose one." I chose to be the solution. That was my breakthrough moment!

Coming To Canada

My husband and I made a critical decision to relocate to Canada to have dual citizenship and expose our children to the Western world. It was a scary decision because I would relocate alone before my family joined me. We had only been married for five years, and God had kept us together, not just as husband and wife but also as friends and lovers. Fear gripped my heart when I thought about moving abroad alone because I would start all over again to find a balance in a new country and society without my dear husband. The system wasn't working well in Nigeria. I was on a journey for greener pastures, so I buckled up.

I initially went to Ontario to study for my postgraduate degree. However, two days later, on January 2, 2015, I moved to Saskatchewan as that province had a more accessible immigration pathway to becoming a permanent resident. The struggle for survival and attainment of purpose began all over again. I needed to get my tuition back from the college I initially registered in. The day I was supposed to travel from Saskatoon to Sarnia, Ontario, to get a refund of my school fees, I had a clear vision not to embark on the journey because I saw a plane crash. I tried to change the ticket or get my money back, but I couldn't, so I decided to travel despite the ominous warning. I didn't want to waste my ticket fare. However, the night flight I was supposed to board was moved to the following morning due to the bad weather forecast for flying. I praised God, hoping that He had averted a calamity for me. The next day, I boarded the plane to Toronto, hoping to reach my destination, Sarnia in Ontario. About thirty-five minutes after takeoff, I noticed tension on the face of the co-pilot because it was a small plane, and we could all see each other. Suddenly, everything went blank, and nothing was displayed on the dashboard. I panicked and started pleading for God's mercy and intervention. The pilot announced that the plane had a mechanical fault, but he managed to land it safely. God saved me, His disobedient child. I believed He rescued me because my mission on earth was not accomplished yet. I vowed to myself never to disobey Him again.

In Saskatchewan, I studied at the Saskatoon Business College. After obtaining my diploma as a Clinical Administrative Assistant, I received an eighteen-month work permit, which meant I had to get a full-time job in my designated field and acquire my stipulated working hours before applying for permanent residency. I was pressed for time because of my immigration timeline, so I searched for a job earnestly. One day, I printed twenty copies of my resume and walked from one clinic to another, searching for a job. Finally, I entered a skin clinic to submit my resume, and the receptionist on duty said: "We have no vacancy, and even if we did, we wouldn't take someone of your skin colour."

I was devastated! I could not believe that my skin colour was working against me. No doubt, that was a racist remark! What does my colour have to do with my abilities and capabilities? Oh my! I was highly discouraged but determined to continue the fight. After three weeks, I got a casual job with a clinic. I gave the job my all, and my manager loved my dedication and hard work. However, they did not have space for a permanent position. One day, my manager requested my resume, perused it again, and forwarded it to another clinic. She asked me to apply, and long and behold, I got the job!

I explained my immigration status to the new clinic manager, and she was willing to help. Surprisingly, she started the process the following day. I owe her! I was the only black employee in that clinic, and I vowed to prove to anyone with negative perceptions or opinions about my colour and race wrong. I wanted to change the stereotypes against Nigerians and Africans as a whole. I was available and reliable. Sometimes, I would be the only staff assisting the doctors when other staff were absent. I was efficient as a clinic assistant and as an office administrator. I gave the role the best of me. I was loved by the doctors, my co-workers, and the patients - they considered me to be a real blessing. A year into the job, I was offered a managerial position. Unfortunately, since my husband was not always at home, and I was often alone with my two children without readily available help, I could not take the job because of the highly demanding responsibilities and long working hours required.

Seeking More Fulfilment

Did I find fulfilment in the job? Well, I STILL HAD MORE TO OFFER AND MORE WITHIN ME. So, I embarked on a journey to find more satisfaction and what I wanted to do. First, I opened a Facebook account and started a YouTube channel to discuss social and religious issues. I discuss moral values, educate younger generations about life, and interview professionals. I named the platform In Between I Stand to reach Christians, Muslims, and all colours and races, young and old.

The name I chose became a problem for those who needed help understanding my purpose. I became a topic for sermons, where I heard comments such as: "You cannot be hot and cold, you must stand for something, and you cannot be in-between." But I developed a resolute mindset about what I wanted and learned to put people's opinions aside. I remained steadfast and allowed nothing to move me. I had chosen to be a ' solution' and not a 'problem'. The opinion of others was no longer a problem for me. I am a strong African woman who has a clear destination in mind. The bridges, the curves, and the potholes made my story bulky, but the naysayers could not stop me. I will share more about this experience in my book, which will be published soon.

I worked on my self-development by attending seminars, lectures, and programs for leadership training and public speaking organised by Fela Durotoye, Mary Akpobome, and many others. I invested in my growth and intellect. My hope was heightened again. I hired a coach to enlighten me and help me create a balance in my numerous endeavours. I studied the experiences of successful Black women. I constantly reminded myself that I am the solution and can be anything I want to be if I put my mind and effort into it.

I took another bold step to return to school in the desired field to realize my dream of becoming a Marriage Therapist/Counselor. I gained admission to study psychology at the University of Saskatchewan. I registered at another institute simultaneously to obtain my certification in relationship coaching. One day, I received an email about the Saskatchewan Leadership Training Program. I submitted my profile and was selected to attend. "Do you think I'm doing too much?" Well, I had to do what I had to do. I had enough of what people thought I should be doing, and it was high time I focused on my dreams and goals!

Ultimately, I took all the negativity people threw at me and used it as a stepping stone for my dreams. Some wanted to stop me by throwing stones, but I used them to build. I'm thankful for the stones on which I have built my motivation freely. I am the owner of Ibiss Natural Wellness, which offers seven skin care products. I am a certified relationship coach and the founder of IBISS LOVE HAVEN, where I coach singles and married people with relationship issues. I am also studying psychology at the University of Saskatchewan. I am growing and building, and there's more within me.

The Good Mirror

I want to be a mirror that people can look up to and draw strength from. A mirror that encourages, a mirror that leads the way, a mirror that relieves the broken, a reflective mirror of hope, strength, power, audacity, courage, fearlessness, purpose, determination, and self-discovery. I am on a journey, and this is just the beginning of my story.

Now I invite every lady to remember that you can make an impact with whatever you have in your hands. You have a solution to someone's problem. Your colour is your heritage, and your race is your pride. You don't have to be perfect or a finished product to effect change and influence your community; even if you're broken, you can still rise. A broken pencil writes; you need to sharpen it! Remember the statement that tortured me for years "A jack of all trades is a master of none!" I now believe it's better to be a master of many than to be a master of only one! So many people battle imposter syndrome, a common phenomenon. However, I am a testimony that you can overcome it and pursue your dreams. I hope that my story has inspired you to never give up on your purpose because of your limiting beliefs or the fear of other people's opinions of you.

Meet The Author

Paula Collins-Pingue is the Owner & Director of MASALA Model & Talent & School of Personal Development.

Paula is a Mentor, Motivational Speaker, Stylist, Image Consultant, Model & Acting Coach with 43 years experience in the model and talent industry and is still thriving.

MASALA is the only model, talent and personal development center owned by a Black person in Canada

She creates personal & professional development, life skills programs for children & teens, adults as well as career enhancement lectures, for post secondary institutions & corporate businesses.

Paula has a new business empowering women over the age of thirty-five on health, wellness, beauty, image consulting and more.

Paula is a Black Lives Matter activist and serves on the board of The Black Professionals & Entrepreneurs of Saskatchewan BPES Inc.

To inquire more about MASALA's services
CONTACT:
Email: masalatalent@sasktel.net
PH: +1.306.241.2330
IG: https://www.Instagram.com/masalamodeltalent
FB: https://www.facebook.com/MasalaModelTalent

Paula Collins-Pingue

DO NOT IGNORE YOUR GIFT. YOUR GIFT IS THE THING YOU DO THE ABSOLUTE BEST WITH THE LEAST AMOUNT OF EFFORT.

– Steve Harvey

Chapter 12

THERE'S NOTHING MINOR ABOUT ME!

by Paula Collins-Pingue

I share my heart, my dreams, challenges, faith, and victories in becoming the woman I am today. God has abundantly blessed me with life lessons that have impacted me significantly. He has shielded me from disaster, and I am forever grateful to continue to learn and grow from my experiences. I hope my story will bring you joy and help empower you in any way, no matter your circumstances. In a world and industry that was not fully inclusive, my faith enabled me to challenge my worth and persevere as a leading Black woman in Saskatchewan and worldwide.

Southen Girl!

I was born in Louisville, Mississippi USA, in the Jim Crow South of the early 1960's. My parents were born and raised in the Bluegrass state of Kentucky. My family moved back to Kentucky for a few years until deciding to start a new beginning in Saskatoon, Saskatchewan, Canada, in 1970. My family and I had just arrived at our new home for the first time and as I got out of the car, suddenly a little boy standing on the street started shouting: "The monkeys are coming, the monkeys are coming!" I looked at my brother, bewildered, and wondered where were the monkeys, what monkeys? Until it dawned on me that he was talking about us. We were the monkeys! That very moment I was hurt and felt we were ugly. The church we attended, we were the only Black family and at school, there were only four of us in total which included my brother and I. For the first time, I was conscious that I was different and alone. I longed to be back in Kentucky among my own people and community. My mom suffered from depression, and it became a struggle to adapt to a new life with no support system. My dad created new opportunities on his own for our family, and being self-sufficient, he easily adjusted. I have rarely used the word minority, as I know there's nothing minor about me.

I spoke with a bold southern drawl that had charm and sass. If you rubbed me the wrong way, I'd place my hand on my hip, cut a side eye then roll my eyes. "Don't mess with me!" My brother, Floyd Jr., and I grew up having to defend ourselves, and we were in frequent physical fights at school. We never started the fights but always finished them. We also defended our younger sister, Michelle. We were tired of being called the ugly N-word, Blacky, and other racial slurs that made fun of our beautiful brown skin, backsides, noses, and how we talked. Touching, patting, or pulling my hair was an absolute no-no. "Leave my pressed hair, afro puffs, and plaits alone!" I was not a pet, toy, or plaything for adult strangers or children to touch and caress.

I developed a sense of duty to defend and protect other Black and brown children that didn't have enough confidence to stand up for themselves. I was present and stood with boldness and grace, with a projected voice to be seen and heard even when fearful. These skills have never left me and have served me well in my personal and career life.

Stay Elevated and Know Who You Are

I am from a generation of women who stand united in elevating smart, talented, resilient women who came before us. Unfortunately, we continue to experience the inequities that are inherent to our sociocultural environment. Being a Black woman has added layers of judgement, lack of respect, oppression, insecurity, and anxiety. We are ridiculed, leaving the impression that we are incapable of achieving excellence in anything we do. We have always had to compete against our counterparts instead of being validated for our credentials and contributions. Actress, singer, and entertainer Sheryl Lee Ralph gave a profound speech at the Critics Choice Awards. "People don't have to like you. People don't have to love you. They don't even have to respect you. But when you look in the mirror, you better love what you see. You better love what you see!". YAAASSS HALLELUJERRRR!

Light, Camera, Action!

My family instilled in my heart my love for music and the arts and entertainment industry at a very young age. Coming from a musical family and being an extrovert, who embraced the freedom of self-expression, I came alive on stage. I had no fear of being the centre of attention.

I was scouted at age sixteen by Pizzazz Modeling & Talent Agency while walking the runway during a fashion show. I loved strutting the runway, grooving to the music, and having a beautiful smile. I was the only Black model, and there was one model of E. Indian descent. We were the token models and took every advantage to showcase ourselves and exude elegance and grace, making a lasting impression. I took several courses in personal development, professional modeling, and acting. I was one of the top 10 Saskatchewan models who numerous clients frequently requested. I became a mentor for new faces to build their confidence on the runway and their image. It was an honour to be trusted to assist in their development. I became an emcee filling in last minute for a fashion show when the courier didn't deliver the radio station's voice-over recorded script. I had to go live and improvise the whole performance. What a rush, I was named model of the month.

After high school, I took psychology night classes at the University of Saskatchewan and worked full-time for a year. I then attended Boise State University majoring in Music Education.

At the age of twenty-two, in 1986, I travelled to New York with my director and agency, Pizzazz, and thirty-five eager fellow models, actors, singers, and dancers for an international competition. Although to my disappointment, I was not offered a contract or callbacks, I learned so much, and the experience to this day was life-changing. When you have goals and a vision, stay true to who you are. If you're with the right partner, they will support and encourage you. I married my fiancé in 1987.

I worked with the airlines in 1986 for a few years before having a family. I was based in Calgary and commuted to Saskatoon. I enjoyed being a flight attendant because it allowed me to escape and view the world from a new perspective.

My husband and I were ready to start a family, and I was in Saskatoon full-time. I was back in the fashion and entertainment industry when it was booming in Saskatchewan, booking shows, shoots, and promo events. Fast forward a few years later, I had two young children; I also found myself purchasing my first business, in September 2000, with a partner and then, within a year and a half, being the sole proprietor. I was a businesswoman in this market, promoting models and actors of all ethnicities, ages, and sizes and running training courses for kids and adults. I had to work harder not only for myself but also for the models that trusted me to represent them and manage their careers. I was uncomfortable using my images as the owner for marketing for fear that clients wouldn't hire my company or register for classes. I wasn't confident that people would be okay seeing just my beautiful Black face in an ad. Many people expected me to fail. Having two young children and operating a company intended for two directors was challenging to juggle. My husband was working overtime to make ends meet. I was so grateful to have both parents and in-laws living in the same city to care for the kids and help keep my sanity.

To constantly prove my knowledge, expertise, and worth, I had to show up every day as the ultimate professional—dressing the part, speaking the part, and constantly being on brand. People were watching and continued to watch. I persevered, having lasted over twenty years in this industry, even when the Sask. film employment tax credit ended in 2012, leaving crew and productions to move to larger markets due to lack of funding. As a result, I've had to differentiate my business from others by offering a diverse talent pool.

I also structured the courses I offered and made a point of teaching in areas others weren't considering at the time, such as self-esteem, healthy body image, bullying, public speaking, fashion marketing, business etiquette, peer pressure, and much more. An exciting part of this industry is managing the careers of my models and talent by attending conventions, meeting international scouts and agencies, and placing them nationally and internationally.

My Mentors for Life

My maternal grandmother, Elizabeth Gentry Smith was so special to me. She was highly respected as a leader in her church and community; she was a minister, choir director, and teacher, and she raised a talented musical family. She was loving, nurturing, and funny in a no-nonsense way when talking with the young folks about respecting themselves and respect for their elders. An entire year I lived with her when I was fourteen. Can you imagine living alone with an older woman who was set in her ways and a freshman in junior high going through puberty and coping with peer pressure? I learned to give her insulin needles. I tell you, we were quite a pair, and we became inseparable, living in the projects of Charlotte Court in Kentucky. She gave me guidance in respecting and honouring myself at an impressionable age. We talked a lot, and she wanted to know how I was and how I felt and praised me for achievements in school, sports, bible school, and how I was maturing. I was away from my parents and family, so it helped me develop independence. She taught me how to cook and make the delicious rolls I still make today. I miss her so much.

My big 'sister,' my mentor and influencer in my life until the day she passed away, was my cousin Vannessa. She was a few years older than I. She was my saving grace in my adolescent years right up to becoming a woman and having a family. Vannessa was my confidant, my ride-or-die, and she was my image consultant. In the early days of my business, she guided me, gave me ideas, and encouraged me. I often think of her and what she would do and say. To this day, I hear her voice.

My beautiful parents have been strong role models and mentors for my siblings and me, as well as the youth in our community to adults in organisations, businesses, and the church. They demonstrate leadership, integrity, strength, and pride. Family reunions are essential to remember who we are. They taught me confidence, faith, etiquette, poise, professionalism and to not back down in the face of injustice but rather to fight for what is right. To be proud of my beautiful black skin, to speak the truth, and to project my voice when speaking. My eyes are to look up and direct when addressing and engaging with an audience. I was to command a presence and leave a positive lasting impression. Most of all, I want to keep God first in my life and trust Him explicitly.

My momma taught me the importance of self-care and wellness, which built my confidence and self-worth. She was a former elementary substitute teacher in Kentucky. She became a beauty and fashion consultant at Eaton's for twenty-five years in Saskatoon. Her volunteer work provided care for Hospice patients, Meals on Wheels and facilitated programs for people with mental health. My momma didn't take any mess regarding us kids being bullied at school. She became a regular visitor at the principal's office. There was an incident when a teacher pulled my brother's hair out; momma stormed to the teacher's classroom and told her she would slap the 'taste' out of her mouth if she ever laid another hand on her children. I knew then my momma was fearless!

As for my daddy, I've inherited some of his traits. He's very approachable, outgoing, confident, funny, and has a youthful attitude. He compliments himself in the mirror on how well he's dressed (I don't do that *wink). He's direct and makes no apologies for firm decisions he's made that don't please others. The word obstacles don't exist in his vocabulary or in his life. My dad was a music teacher in Ky, and then he was recruited for the Defensive Backfield football coach position for Cumberland High School in Ky. He brought the team that hadn't won to victory more than three games in a season to reach an impressive all-time high of a 9-1 record. Dad was not permitted to attend the awards banquet claiming it would make the attendees uncomfortable because he was Black! He was hurt but knew what he brought to the team was immeasurable. In Saskatoon, dad became the first Black person at the top of the sales charts across North America for the life insurance and financial planning companies he worked with. My dad is the definition of resilience.

When I think back, whether it is my grandmother, my mom, or my dad, It's that kind of no-nonsense attitude that made an impression on me. My parents' decisions were rooted in their values and faith, so they knew they were doing the right thing. I've continued to live my life in that way. I am fun-loving and want to see the best in everyone I encounter. Sometimes I am firm and direct when speaking of things I am passionate about. Other times people are taken aback by my honesty and candour. As a result, some situations find me defending my worth or my knowledge of a particular problem, which leaves me feeling undermined, disrespected, and other times not seen. Being assertive shows that you respect yourself because you're willing to stand up for your interests and express your thoughts and feelings. It also demonstrates that you know others' rights and are eager to work on resolving conflicts.

Life Is Worth Living!

I recall a very troubling time in my senior year of high school. I was a social butterfly, athletic in various sports, and music activities. I had a great job in fashion, and I seemed to have it all. Unbeknownst to everyone, specifically my family, I was going through depression. There was no isolated reasoning behind it, but I was unhappy. I loved my family dearly, and I had great friends; I was popular, but there was an overwhelming amount of pressure and unhealthy relationships that caused me to spiral, and I lost that sparkle that I once shone.

One evening, I wrote a letter to my parents and siblings, I put it on my night table, and I grabbed a collection of pills from the medicine cabinet. I didn't read the labels; I don't recall how many drugs I put in my hand. I sat on my bed, ingested the pills, then laid down on my pillow and closed my eyes. I asked God to let me rest and take me away. As I drifted, I faintly remember saying I didn't want to die. The next day I woke up feeling very uneasy. I had a headache and was dizzy. I'm sure I asked God why I was still here. I went to school and tried to act as if nothing had happened. When I reached my locker, one of my dear friends told me I looked like crap. "What's wrong with you, Paula?" She asked. "You don't look well," I confessed to her. "I took some pills last night." She hugged me and walked me to the counsellors office to allow me to go home from school. My friend invited me to her home and took care of me for the day.

Thank goodness God spared my life. He was not ready for me. I felt guilty, wondering how my actions would have devastated my family if anything had happened to me. My mom asked me a few days later if I had taken any of her pills. I lied and said no. For decades I never spoke of this to anyone other than my husband and daughter. I guess God had plans for my life in a way I could impact others from the pain I had suffered. I have been transparent on social media about anxiety and depression. I am so grateful that I have been blessed to have amazing support personally and in business.

I've always felt compassion for people with low self-esteem, the youth, and people who want to feel more confident. God has given me a gift to empower, motivate, and believe that anything in life is possible. If you stay faithful and surround yourself with good people who have your very best interest at heart, you can achieve anything.

What It Takes!

As a business, it's all about service. Provide what the client needs and build a great partnership with a lasting relationship and referrals. In my industry, as a model and talent agent, I provide professionals, new face models, and actors to be the face of a brand, to advertise a product for consumers, to model garments and beauty products, provide street teams and brand ambassadors to create awareness of products and to portray characters and voices to tell a story. It takes a great attitude, willingness to learn, commitment, and lots of practice. I train my talent to be knowledgeable in their craft and apply themselves confidently, providing the proper tools to be their best.

I'm not just their agent; I also view myself as a mentor and manager who guides and champions them. As a free spirit, creative, and not necessarily structured in how I approach business and life, I pride myself on being approachable, authentic, fun, and focused on nurturing people. You could say that I don't have time for people who are fake or standoffish. Just as people say, "don't judge a book by its cover," don't judge me because I don't work the same way you do or in a "corporate-like" way. For example, I can speak about confidence, self-worth, and overcoming mental health difficulties to a large group and motivate them from experience. Although some require weeks of preparation, I can be spontaneous. I let my authenticity shine through; many have told me they consider me a good leader.

As for me, I consider myself a winner because I've had joy in seeing others grow and succeed and learn from my impact on their lives. Of course, my success hasn't always been monetary, but it returns to my agency and me more when I serve others.

I am proud to be a facilitator of Black Girls Arise, a seven-month course in mentoring Black Girls ages 7-18. This program is empowering in developing our next generation of leaders. Global Empowerment Initiative for Women Inc. is one of our sponsors.

Boss Up, Be Recognized and Take Risks

I remember a very profound lesson that my cousin Vannessa had told me frequently with her sweet Southern voice and finger twirling in the air, "Gurl, don't you worry about what other people say about you; you are critical to be the topic of their conversation". "Shooooot, I wish somebody would talk about me." We would bust out laughing and hug each other.

Know who you are and what you stand for. Trust your intuition when others offer advice only to make themselves comfortable in their skin. You are unique, and not everyone will support your beliefs. Setting boundaries is vital, so you don't lose yourself and your worth.

Your overall image is everything from how you dress, talk, walk, personal hygiene, demeanor, speaking skills, eye contact, and etiquette. First impressions make a lasting impression. So here s a few questions for you: "How memorable are you? What do you want people to say about you? Do you know to showcase yourself in a conversation with a group? How are your etiquette skills? What do you see in the mirror? Do you love what you see? Do you love what you do? Who do you aspire to be? Who are you giving services to, and is it excellent service? Are you good to yourself and loving on yourself?" You deserve to be loved and supported. It's time to celebrate you and all that you are now and will become in the future. Nothing nor no one can stop you from what God's plans are for you—NOTHING! You are beautiful! You are Special! You are Fierce! You are Amazing! You are smart! You are talented! You are loved. I LOVE YOU!

I have learned to take risks. If you are unwilling to take risks, I don't know how you can ever become a leader. Taking risks also means handling rejection in a way that allows you to learn from it. You have to be able to ask yourself: "Why the rejection? Was it because you didn't perform well? Because people needed more time to be ready for you, your message, or your service? Wasn't it the right timing?" Or you weren't the right person for the task, either because it wasn't a project that you really believed in or you weren't educated enough to be able to do the work. Regardless, taking risks and rejection go hand in hand sometimes, and you have to be able to handle both.

In the same mindset, you also have to be able to handle mistakes. I've made many mistakes and will continue to, but it doesn't mean I'm a failure. It just means I need to get back up again and try better. Confidence sets you apart from the rest when stepping out in faith. At times you may be the first to do something new. Set goals and write out your affirmations to strive to make your dreams become realities. Believe in who you are, recognize your gifts and talents, and clarify your purpose. Don't give up—ever!

I had encountered many women who have been strong supporters and advocated for me when I was young, starting as a model and later with my business. I particularly recall when my former business partner left after a year and a half of opening the agency; it was a trying time financially and emotionally. A group of amazing women who were mothers of some of my talent and my church family came to my aid and empowered me to see the good I was doing. They were inspiring, prayed over me, and helped me regain my confidence to move forward to be the best ambassador I could be for the business.

No matter the stage of my life, I have had some amazing people around me, and there are many more to this day. I am so thankful that God put them on my path. I have come to realize that in life, like in business, having role models to look up to and emulate and a strong support group, whether they are family or friends, is valuable. I consider myself a great friend, supporter, cheerleader, sister in love, and advocate.

GOD Is My Constant in Everything!

Faith plays a significant role in my perseverance in business, follow-through, and my private life. My faith guides my decisions, my trust in people to listen, and my follow-through.

Professionalism has allowed me to demonstrate that I can be a confident, smart black woman who is reliable and skilled. That same professionalism has helped me brand my agency not only in ownership but in the talent that I represent and the clients that I serve. Yes, I bring some exoticism and use my platform to advocate for black and brown models with ethnic hair and traditional styles and clothing. Being an all-inclusive agency, I'm proud to showcase everything we are in celebrating one's authentic self. My professionalism, faith, and confidence have helped me be part of the change I wanted to see in our industry, which is a form of MASALA, meaning—'Exotic mixtures of Spice,' that's actually what the world is made up of.

Being Authentic Is Key!

Leadership also realizes when you need to take a break from what you usually do and focus on yourself. I once took an eight-month break from social media and promoting my business. I wasn't in a good place and needed to recharge again. During that time, I had many people—particularly women and a few men—who noticed my absence, reached out to me and offered their support, and welcomed me back with open arms when I was ready. Taking this break taught me that I don't have to be scared to ask for help, lean on people when I need it, share my story, and be vulnerable. Honestly, I thrive on sisterhood and on spending time with other women of all cultures and statuses. I also love my guys; there're some real ones, and I adore them. I take opportunities to attend events to network, support and unwind from a long week, being with some of the people already in my sphere and others that might develop into friendships or not, and that's okay too. I joined a team of professionals and entrepreneurs in a high-level personal development program to guide, support, and mentor me daily. Aligning yourself with like-minded individuals to be accountable for your success in everything you do for your family and business is crucial. Top mentors, successful leaders, and entrepreneurs are mentored by someone more knowledgeable and capable to help elevate their mindset. Surround yourself with people who are sincerely motivated and invested in your success and possibly more than you are. You may also be a great mentor to someone while you are on your journey to a successful career.

I am so fortunate to have amazing talented models, actors, and talent that have been featured in numerous fashion events and acting projects across the globe. It's gratifying to seem them in magazines, local and national films, TV projects, campaigns, and shows. Masala is all about community: providing in-kind sponsorship is another way for my agency to be genuine in building and supporting our community annually. Also, my models and talent enjoy donating their time by participating in various charities, award banquets, galas, and inner-city communities, to name a few. I have received calls for paid engagements because people noticed us at an event. So, when I think of leadership, I believe it's also about being visible and part of the community in any way you can. It's good for my soul, and as it turns out, it is also suitable for business.

I was honored to be a representative of the City of Saskatoon's Cultural Unit in collaboration with the Peoples Bridge Advocacy. This opportunity contributed to the City's first formal engagement with systemic barriers within the Black community.

I realized that being a business leader and trying to thrive in other areas that matter to me don't always go hand in hand. In 2016 I started advocating for Black Lives Matter and helped plan and lead the first ever peaceful march in Saskatchewan. I realized that for some people, that was 'too much.' Demonstrating my values and beliefs, I have been told that I am 'too radical, too black, too outspoken, too opinionated, too confident in my people!' Wow! It made some people uncomfortable for non-blacks and blacks. But I pressed on because it meant that there was a lot more work that needed to be done for people to accept that racism still exists. It's time to accept each others uniqueness and beauty. We also need to accept and affirm ourselves.

When I'm blessed to wake up in the morning, I will still be that amazing, fierce, confident woman who is making a significant mark in her community, developing confidence and wellness by showcasing beauty and diversity worldwide. I don't have to defend myself; I will continue to be proud and hopefully leave a legacy for the next generations, who will live fully and unapologetically. So be that boss that takes leaps of faith in slaying the naysayers. At the end of the day, when I look in the mirror, I love what I see. I love that I have made a positive impact and will continue to. "Paula, you are an amazing, relevant trailblazer and adored. You go, gurl!"

Scripture

"Now faith is the substance of things hoped for, the evidence of things not seen"
– Hebrews 11:1 KJV

"For we walk by faith, not by sight."
– 1 Corinthians 5:7 NKJV

"'For I know the plans I have for you," declares the Lord, "plans to prosper you and not to harm you, plans to give you hope and a future.'"
– Jeremiah 29:11

AMEN!

Acknowledgements

To my gurl Betty Mutwiri, you were there for me when I first started my business, praying for and with me through tough times and celebrating my triumphs. We've been through a lot together and I am so proud of you for showing a exemplary example of what leadership, sisterhood, class and excellence truly means. Thank you for encouraging me to finish my story, I am so grateful. May God continue to bless you always.

TO MY LOVES!

My story is dedicated to my big sister, Vannessa Ann Smith, my ride or die, the most beautiful soul. Forever love and adore you sissy, smooches all over your face. Till we're together again.

My biggest advocate, support system, angel investor, sounding board, confident, and closest friend—my husband Hugh Pingue. He has been giving me grace, humbly accepting me, allowing me to be vulnerable and propping me for over forty years. In business and at home he is my rock. Together, we have built a strong and loving family. Our daughter, Jasmyn, and son Jadyn are our greatest pride and joy. I am particularly grateful for my daughter now working with me, helping our family business thrive and my son using his God given gifts on the football field and in school. My parents, Floyd Sr. and Bettye Collins, my brother, Floyd Jr, sister Michelle, I'm grateful for their love and support throughout my life. None of what I do would mean the same without any of them. They are my life and my world.

LOVE YOU,
PAULA

”

IF YOU CAN SEE IT IN YOUR MIND, YOU CAN HOLD IT IN YOUR MIND

– Steve Harvey

Meet The Author

Betty Mutwiri is the Principal of BM Leadership Coaching and Consulting Inc. when she partners with organisational leaders across Canada and beyond to maximize their leadership impact, navigate complex change and increase employee engagement. She does this through executive coaching, leadership development programs and Equity, Diversity & Inclusion (EDI) strategy development. She leverages her two-decade senior leadership experience to provide insightful results-oriented strategies. She also acts as an Adjunct and Associate Faculty for various academic programs.

Betty is a proud Kenyan-Canadian, mother and wife. She is passionate about unleashing people's potential and mentoring the next generation of leaders. She developed the transformative 3A Coach-Approach Model as a co-author of *ROOTED: A Mentoring Journey*, published by Sisterhood Ministries. Betty also founded the BIPOC Leadership Academy to accelerate the development of BIPOC leaders. She is the project lead and lead author of the collaborative book project, *Courage, Change & Faith*, by Black Women Leaders SK.

Betty was named one of Canada's Top 100 Black Women to Watch in 2022 and she received the Queen Elizabeth II Platinum Jubilee Medal in recognition of her positive contribution to the province of Saskatchewan, Canada.

https://www.linkedin.com/in/betty-mutwiri
https://bmcoachingconsulting.ca/
https://bipocleadershipacademy.ca/

Betty Mutwiri

MA, PCC, Ph.D.c

FOR I CAN DO EVERYTHING THROUGH CHRIST, WHO GIVES ME STRENGTH.

Philippians 4:13 NLT

Chapter 13

PURPOSE, POTENTIAL & POWER

by Betty Mutwiri

What lies before us and what lies behind us
are tiny matters to what lies within us.
– Ralph Waldo Emerson

A series of changes and serendipitous events have characterized my life. These changes have helped me discover my purpose, maximize my potential and ignite my inner power. Before each new leadership move, I sense inner restlessness followed by a period of active discernment. I then take action and meet kindred spirits on my adventure. We may encounter steep hills that call for immense stamina to ascend. These deep valleys test our endurance and bubbling brooks that replenish our weary souls and spirit. I was drawn to the quote, "what lies before us and what lies behind us are tiny matters to what lies within us," as it captures the essence of what has initiated and informed most of my leadership adventures. What lies within refers to the inner force that I find too compelling to ignore and what becomes a fountain of wisdom that helps me navigate a life of uncertainty. In my opinion, leadership is not an event but a way of life; it's a choice to step up and step out in response to a need or to act as a change catalyst to bring into being initiatives that positively impact people.

My Early Years

My family lived in a small rural community on the northern slopes of Mt. Kenya. As the only girl in a family with four brothers, I grew up sandwiched between two older and two younger brothers. Being the only girl in the family, I spent much time alone reading. My passion for reading also helped me perform well in school, which pleased my parents. My father constantly reminded us that education was the pathway to a better life and motivated us to work hard by promising to buy a gift for whoever brought a good report card at the end of the school term. Dangling that carrot intensified my efforts as I enjoyed the reward of a new pair of shoes or a new dress at the end of each term. That passion transcended the early years as I still consider myself a lifelong learner.

I am inspired by how my parents curated a life designed around their aspirations of providing a “good life” for their children and then worked diligently and with great persistence toward that. They both had a vibrant entrepreneurial spirit which led them to build a small fortune for themselves in a relatively short time. They also believed in making lemonade when life tossed them lemons. They were tenacious, and their ‘can do’ attitude helped them achieve their goals. These qualities left an imprint on me and have significantly influenced my life.

It wasn’t all work and no play! A fun bonding family activity was storytelling before bedtime when my mother would gather us around the fire. I looked forward to these times with much anticipation. My mother enhanced her delivery by adding suspense and drama. I recall one folktale of a hyena invited to two parties and could not decide which one to attend. When he arrived at the crossroads, he placed one foot on each path, and as the paths continued to diverge, he split in half!! While that might sound ridiculous, the underlying lesson against greed has always stuck with me. Our cultural tradition passed down the values and virtues through storytelling, and I am still enthralled with the practice!

Every child needs a hero. One of my childhood heroes was my maternal grandmother, Helen. She was compassionate, joy-filled and loving, which made her beautiful brown eyes sparkle! I fondly recall her warm hospitality whenever we visited on Sunday afternoons—she would insist on spoiling us despite her meagre means. She also had a way of making me feel 'seen' and valued. The following quote by Maya Angelou, "people don't care how much you know until they see how much you care," reminds me of my grandma's essence. While she transitioned from this earth, she still inspires me to live a life of joy irrespective of the circumstances and genuinely love and care for people. Positive emotions are contagious!

Despite being the only girl in a culture that privileged male children, I never felt 'less than' because I was a female. Credit to my father, who helped nurture my confidence and courage by giving me challenging responsibilities. His trust in me grew with each stretch experience such that upon his demise (bless his soul), he left me responsible for a few roles, which unfortunately unleashed intense backlash. The lack of continuity of his values and legacy has caused me much heartache. However, the experience has taught me that cultural values run deep, and counter-cultural change can be messy and longstanding.

New Beginnings

In 1992, I relocated to Canada to join my husband, who was already studying in Ontario, Canada. While there, we were blessed with our daughter, Vanessa. Upon my husband's graduation, we moved to San Diego where we welcomed our son, George Jr., sixteen months after our daughter was born. Nine years later, our last son Gitonga was born. Becoming a mama was a life-changing experience. The memory of beholding my babies still evokes tender emotions of joy and gratitude. I thank God every day for the privilege of being their mother. They are precious to me; each has taught me so much about myself.

My husband and I experienced a spiritual awakening during our time in San Diego. This happened thanks to a lovely couple, Michael, and Betsy Brown, whom we met while shopping in the mall one sunny afternoon. Later, they pursued a friendship with us over several months and invited us to their church. They soon became our extended family of choice and connected us to a supportive community of friends. One thing that made me curious about this couple was their selfless service and joy. My soul yearned for this. So, one day I asked Betsy: "What's the secret to your joy." I was curious because despite having married the man of my dreams and having two healthy and beautiful kids, there was still a longing within my soul. She gave me a big smile and said: "How about I help you forge a relationship with Jesus Christ." While I had grown up in a Christian household, I was not practicing my faith through the spiritual disciplines of prayer, meditation, and reading scripture. So, I decided to give it a shot while she played a mentoring role. Eventually, I integrated these practices into my daily and weekly rhythms. I also started to feel more grounded, joyful, and peaceful. Undoubtedly, this was a significant turning point in my life. Nurturing my faith was a game-changer! The spiritual illumination I achieved transformed my perspective on life and gave me the inner strength and the wisdom to navigate the transitions that followed soon after.

After three short years in San Diego, my husband got a job in western Canada, and it was time to pack our bags again. Soon after we arrived in Saskatoon, I came across two books by Steven Covey, T*he Seven Habits of Highly Effective People* and *First Things First*. These books stirred a passion for personal development and values-based leadership. They guided me in developing my vision, mission, and values. I could reflect on who I wanted to be and identify what was important to me during a vulnerable transition. I was grateful for the opportunity to reflect and envision the future I dreamed about as a young girl in Meru. I had a new opportunity to paint bold strokes of colour that reflected my vision, mission, and value statements on a fresh canvas. The prospect was both intimidating and freeing!

Fueled by the energy from these guiding statements, I soon met a lady with whom we decided to establish a non-profit organisation. The purpose of the social enterprise was to foster social and economic empowerment amongst foreign-trained professionals who had recently relocated to Saskatoon. We developed a mandate that attracted a reasonably large membership base. However, after a few years, challenging interpersonal dynamics began to derail the organisation, which led to its ultimate demise. It was a painful loss that I grieved for some time. However, that experience taught me the importance of aligning competing personal agendas in a diverse team and addressing signs of derailment early and decisively.

My second major adventure in Saskatoon, which followed closely at the heels of the first leadership 'failure' was an entrepreneurial business venture. I noted a recurrent theme in the news that local employers found recruiting and retaining foreign-trained professionals challenging because of the lack of spousal and family support during the transition process. Since I had encountered similar challenges, I felt equipped to provide potential solutions. I researched possible business models that offered holistic relocation services in larger centers and approached the Saskatchewan Regional Economic Development Authority (SREDA) to see how I could assist. The then CEO was enthusiastic about the idea. I then founded International Placement Services Inc (IPS Inc.), the first relocation service, which formed a strategic alliance with SREDA. The business grew, and within a year, it expanded its services to rural towns. In 2001, three years after addressing the clear need in Saskatchewan's urban and rural centers, the provincial government decided to adopt my business model and offer it as a public service to support the Saskatchewan Immigrant Nominee Program (SINP). I was pleased to transfer the model to the government, as it had the resources to serve more people. I was also thrilled that the humble idea that emerged from my experience relocating to Saskatoon ended up helping those who came after me under similar circumstances.

The experience with IPS Inc. was pivotal in helping me learn to trust my inner prompt and step out in faith, believing that the right people and other resources will align to help transform the idea into a meaningful reality.

After my season with IPS Inc., I transitioned into the Executive Director role at Leadership Saskatoon. I was excited about the new opportunity in a new sector but faced a steep learning curve. I also battled imposter syndrome for the first time. For example, during one of the graduation ceremonies, the then Board Chair thanked me for achieving stellar results, which prompted a standing ovation from the audience. While I appreciated the gesture, it also triggered an emotional roller coaster for several days. Instead of relishing the moment wholeheartedly, the anxiety of not being able to raise the bar higher in the future terrified me. I realized later that the phenomenon is prevalent among high achievers, who find it difficult to accept their accomplishments and question their right to deserve accolades. I frequently witness the phenomenon in my coaching practice with leaders from all walks of life. So, if you are currently battling it, know that you are not alone, and do not allow it to hold you back.

Another critical lesson I gained while working at Leadership Saskatoon was the importance of gaining cultural intelligence or the ability to function effectively in various cultural contexts. I recall an incident at a board meeting when the members did not engage or ask questions when I presented my monthly report. The response made me uncomfortable, but I was clueless about what to do. Fortunately, one board member who soon became my informal mentor arranged to meet with me for lunch. During our conversation, she asked me to share my thoughts regarding the meeting. Afterward, she gently explained the gaps and gave me tips on strengthening my future delivery. I was highly grateful for her mentorship as it gave me insight into the 'unwritten rules' of the new culture. Her investment in my success inspired me greatly. Years later, I decided to pay it forward by mentoring young women who tapped on my shoulder or to whom I felt drawn. As my mentoring and coaching practice grew, I was inspired to develop a transformative mentoring model that incorporated an 'inquiry' approach. I witnessed my clients gain clarity, agency, and confidence when I held space and provoked their thoughts with powerful questions. As I created the model, the Founder of Sisterhood Ministries invited me to collaborate on the ROOTED mentoring program; this is an example of serendipitous events in my life that synergize to create something bigger beyond my initial imagination. Since 2020, the model has facilitated hundreds of conversations between mentors and mentees, transforming lives.

Being involved in the ROOTED mentoring program by Sisterhood Ministries is very fulfilling. I give God all the glory for the fruit that has come out of it.

Life-long Learning: a Great Companion

My life is my greatest teacher but pursuing formal education has also been invaluable. As my interest in leadership development grew, I sought more knowledge, skills, and tools to serve my clients with excellence. This led me to enroll for a Master of Arts degree in Leadership, followed by a Graduate Certificate in Executive Coaching. I am currently in a doctoral program in Educational Leadership, and I participate in ongoing professional development related to my craft. Expanding my knowledge, skills and toolbox has opened doors to more opportunities, influence, and impact. For example, my academic preparation in leadership and organisation development prepared me for the role of organisational development consultant at the Saskatoon Health Region. Over the period of nine years, I first progressed to Manager of Learning and Leadership, then Director of Organisational Learning and Leadership and Patient & Family Centered Care (PFCC). The ability to work in my area of passion and strength was a huge privilege. I enjoyed the challenges and responsibilities that came with these roles.

I was fortunate to serve under visionary, dynamic and supportive female leaders who allowed my creativity and strategic thinking abilities to flourish. I also led a team of highly skilled organisational development consultants committed to achieving exceptional results. Together, we designed and implemented several projects locally, regionally and provincially. One of my most notable career highlights during this season was the creation and successful launch of the Saskatchewan Leadership Program (SLP) for healthcare leaders, which significantly impacted the leadership culture at a time when the healthcare system was undergoing several transformational changes. The idea of developing a province-wide program came to me after reflecting on our success in delivering two Leadership and Succession Development programs at a regional level, which received an award from the Saskatchewan Association of Health organisations (SAHO) of Excellence. Upon reflecting on the factors that made the programs highly successful, I felt empowered to propose a provincial-wide program that would serve more leaders and maximize the overall system efficiency and effectiveness. Fortunately, the proposal was well received and fully supported by my then vice president, my team, and the provincial funding body. It was an ambitious and exciting project that required intense planning and coordination of several moving parts with the other thirteen health regions. We decided to frame the leadership program on LEADS in a Caring Environment model. As an early adopter of the LEADS framework, I worked closely with Dr. Graham Dickson, professor emeritus of Royal Roads University, who encouraged me to publish my first journal article, which planted the seed for taking doctoral studies. Now, as a certified LEADS Coach, Consultant and Facilitator, I draw from my experiences during this time to inform my work with clients across Canada. The opportunity to work in this sector is highly rewarding.

Passion for Inclusive Leadership

The brutal murder of George Floyd in May 2020 and the racial atrocities against BIPOC (Black, Indigenous, People of Colour) in USA and Canada shook me to the core. As a Black woman, mother, and wife, I felt extreme sadness and anguish over the rising attacks against Black and Brown people. I was utterly shocked and dismayed for weeks and months following George Floyd's death. Eventually, I decided to do something positive to stop the downward spiral. I started by reaching out to a small, diverse group of friends for 'sense-making' conversations. Next, I hosted a virtual book club, where we reviewed books such as *How to be an anti-racist* by Ibrahim Kendi, *White Fragility* by Robin D'Angelo and *Daring Greatly* by Brene Brown. The honest dialogues in these sessions expanded my perspective and sparked a desire to continue hosting forums that would bridge differences and foster cross-cultural understanding. Martin Luther King Jr's proclamation that "Injustice anywhere is a threat to justice everywhere. We are caught in an inescapable network of mutuality, tied in a single garment of destiny," continued to ring true in my soul and constantly reminded me of our shared humanity.

My children and the next generation became my greatest sources of inspiration while I was ruminating on ways to facilitate greater understanding across differences. My daughter's compassionate soul rubbed off on me. My son's strategic and sharp mind led him to launch the Black Medical Student Association Chapter at his university to influence a more inclusive curriculum for medical students. His actions challenged me. My other son's sense of justice inspired me. Together, they led me to explore strategic ways to add value and foster inclusion. Rich Villodas' words reflected my growing edge:

> [...] a culture of moral outrage often creates greater antagonism because the result is not shalom (peace) but self-serving catharsis. Lament, on the other hand, is a feeling of action motivated by compassion rather than catharsis. It requires us to take the pain we see and feel and open ourselves to how God might have us respond.[20]

As I contemplated these words in the Fall of 2020, I received a call from the Executive Director of Global Empowerment Initiative for Women International (GEIWI) Inc. She enquired whether I would be willing to design and deliver a leadership and mentorship program for Black Women. I welcomed this as an opportunity to channel my energy positively by equipping Black women with a strength-based leadership program that would enhance their agency and empower them to reach their desired goals. Additionally, I was excited to facilitate the development of a cohort of Black women leaders for the first time in my twenty-year career. The uptake of the program was remarkable. I delivered the program virtually to comply with the COVID-19 restrictions. Despite the virtual format, the energy created among the participants was palpable. The women exuded confidence and grit. At the graduation ceremony, as each lady shared the impact the program had had on them, I felt immense gratitude for having had the opportunity to enrich their lives positively. I was to accelerate the positive momentum we had created by collaborating on another initiative.

Thus, in my closing remarks, I invited the women to join me in a collaborative book project where we would share our leadership experiences. Half of the women in the cohort enthusiastically signed up. What a delight! We then embarked on this book project inspired and united by the words of the Nigerian author, Chimamanda Adichie, in her famous TEDx, "The danger of a single story". We challenged ourselves to take responsibility for amplifying our stories as Black women leaders.

Another serendipitous moment that aligned with my growing passion for fostering inclusion and equity happened in the summer of 2022. One day, I felt an urgent need to reach out to a colleague at LEADS Canada. I followed through, and lo and behold, she responded immediately and told me she was also thinking of reaching out to me. As I shared my idea of developing an EDI-informed learning opportunity, I could sense her excitement from the other end of the line! Call it synchronicity, serendipity, or a 'Kairos' moment—I am always amazed at how this voice from within knows how and when to initiate something that ends up being more than I could ever fathom. I could share several similar stories, but for now, I hope to have shared enough to illustrate my firm believe in the power and precision of our inner GPS to guide us on uncertain terrains.

Parting thoughts

I hope my story inspires you to harness what lies within you to ignite your purpose, potential and power to flourish and make a difference in other people's lives. That ability exists in all of us. Our shared humanity demands that we all take our place and contribute positively in ways aligned with our unique leadership DNA. Choosing to transform our limiting beliefs and evolve into our highest self and build an ecosystem that enriches our collective good is critical.

Recently, when I was named one of the Top 100 Black Women to Watch by Canada International Black Women Excellence (CIBWE) I celebrated this achievement with my family and friends. This acknowledgement validated the vision I developed when I arrived in Saskatoon in 1997— to live a life of influence and impact grounded on my faith. A few months later, I received the Queen Elizabeth II Platinum Jubilee Medal for my contributions to the province of Saskatchewan, Canada. Upon receiving the medal, my younger son commented: "Mom, you have come full circle." I don't know about this but I am grateful for all the opportunities my home of choice, Treaty Six Territory and the Homeland of the Metis, has brought me.

I am deeply grateful to God and for the divinely ordained helpers who support and nurture my leadership: my husband, George, my adorable children, Vanessa, George Jr, Gitonga and all the beautiful friends, mentors, colleagues and faith community—a few of whom I introduced in these pages and others too many to mention.

In *Lead with Wisdom: How Wisdom Transforms Good Leaders into Great Leaders,* Mark Strom stated that to flourish in a rapidly changing world, we need each other and the wisdom that grows from living wholeheartedly; reflecting on each experience to teach us more about who we are. I fully resonate with that statement and can attest that practicing wisdom has helped my leadership and my life.

Now, I invite you to reflect on the following questions:

What is tugging deep within you?

What is holding you back?

How can you take the first step?

If not you, who?

If not now, when?"

NOTES AND REFERENCES

Notes

Chapter 1
1. Aaron Sansoni: "Live by design, not by default." Jan 1, 2019

Chapter 2
2. https://www.forbes.com, accessed July 2, 2022.
3. Desmond Tutu. https://www.brainyquote.com, accessed July 7, 2022
3. https://www.quotespedia.org/authors/b/brian-tracy/become-the-kind-of-leader-that-people-would-follow-voluntarily-even-if-you-had-no-title-or-position-brian-tracy
5. Buchan, John. https://www.askideas.com, accessed July 2, 2022.5
5. Angelou, Maya. https://www.brainyquote.com, accessed July 10, 2022.6
6. Thomas, Gary. Sacred Influence, Zondervan, Grands Rapids, 2006.
7. Sheri Dew. https://www.goodreads.com, accessed July 15, 2022.
8. Maya Angelou. https://www.brainyquote.com, accessed July 20, 2022
9. Miller, Alice. https://www.brainyquote.com, accessed August 25, 2022.

Chapter 3
12. Coach LaMonte. "YouDay: Lessons from the first Black president". 2022.

Chapter 5
11. https://www.goodreads.com/quotes/5934-i-ve-learned-that-people-will-forget-what-you-said-people, accessed January 30, 2023.

12. Sutton, M. (2020, June 4). *The most empowering Michelle Obama quotes about using your voice to fight for injustice and equality.* Retrieved August 15, 2022, from https://www.goodhousekeeping.com/uk/lifestyle/a32767586/empowering-michelle-obama-quotes/

Chapter 8
13. Hannah Chukwu, "The Kingless People: The Speech Act as Shield and Sword," in *Igbo in the Atlantic World,* eds. Toyin Falola and Raphael Chijioke Njoku. Indianapolis: Indiana University Press, 2016, pp.17-27.
14. Dave Ulrich argues that nature and nurture are equally important in our leadership abilities. See: www.hrzone.com/lead/future/dave-ulrich-50-of-who-we-can-become-is-nurture-and-can-be-changed-through-learning
Accessed February 21, 2022
15. https://www.wikihow.com/Be-a-Good-Prefect/ accessed on February 21, 2022

16. https://www.johnmaxwell.com/blog/defining-moments/ accessed on March 30, 2022
17. "You too, Brutus?" This phrase also comes from the genius of Shakespeare. It occurs in his play, Julius Caesar, (Act-III, Scene-I, Lines, 77). Julius Caesar utters this phrase as his last words, addressing his close friend, Brutus, in the play. https://literarydevices.net › et-tu-brute, accessed on May 24, 2022
18. Igbo language is a language predominantly spoken in the Southeastern part of Nigeria.
19. Cite from the Holy Bible, Numbers 32:23 (NJKV).

Chapter 13
20. Villodas, Rich (2021) *The Deeply Formed Life: Five Transformative Values to Root Us in the Way of Jesus,* p.76

References

Chapter 2

Habecker, Eugene B. (2018) *The Softer side of leadership: Essential Soft Skills That Transform Leaders and the People They Lead.* Sisters, Oregon, USA Deep River Books

Chapter 6
ONLINE RESOURCES FOR ADHD
1.Children and Adults with Attention Deficit/Hyperactivity Disorder (https://chadd.org)
2. www.additudemag.com
3. Canadian ADHD Resource Alliance CADDRA (https://www.caddra.ca)
4. Canadian Mental Health Association CMHA (https://cmha.ca)

Chapter 13
Covey, S. R. (2004). *The 7 habits of highly effective people: Restoring the character ethic* ([Rev. ed.]). Free Press.
Covey, S. R., Merrill, A. R., & Merrill, R. R. (1994). *First things first: to live, to love, to learn, to leave a legacy.* New York, Simon & Schuster.
Strom, Mark, and O'Reilly Safari, Vendor. *Lead with Wisdom: How Wisdom Transforms Good Leaders into Great Leaders.* 1st ed. 2014. Web.
Villodas, Rich (2021) *The Deeply Formed Life: Five Transformative Values to Root Us in the Way of Jesus*